Blood Runs Cold
on the
Black Side of the Mountain

BLOOD RUNS COLD
ON THE
BLACK SIDE OF THE MOUNTAIN

Based on the True Story of Professional Bear Hunter
Bobby Burris

C.F. GERWE

Algora Publishing
New York

Library of Congress Cataloging-in-Publication Data —

Gerwe, Corinne F.
  Blood runs cold on the black side of the mountain / C.F. Gerwe.
    pages cm
  Includes bibliographical references and index.
    ISBN 978-1-62894-003-9 (soft cover : alk. paper) — ISBN 978-1-62894-004-
6 (hard cover : alk. paper) — ISBN 978-1-62894-005-3 (ebook) 1. Burris, Bobby.
2. Adult children of dysfunctional families—Conduct of life. 3. Criminals—
United States—Biography. 4. Bear hunting—Appalachian Mountains. I. Title.
    RC455.4.F3G47 2013
    616.85'820092—dc23
    [B]
                          2013027274

Cover photo 'A lone boy in the Appalachians' by Jake Metcalf Photography.

Printed in the United States

To my son, Guy Adams

Even there, in the mines, underground, I may find a human heart in another convict and murderer by my side, and I may make friends with him, for even there one may live and love and suffer. One may thaw and revive a frozen heart in that convict, one may wait upon him for years, and at last bring up from the dark depths a lofty soul, a feeling, suffering creature; one may bring forth an angel, create a hero! There are so many of them, hundreds of them, and we are to blame for them.

—Fyodor Dostoevsky, *The Brothers Karamazov*

TABLE OF CONTENTS

CHAPTER ONE

As I crossed the savannah I played with this fancy; but when I reached the ridgy eminence, to look down once more on my new domain, the fancy changed to a feeling so keen that it pierced to my heart and was like pain in its intensity, causing tears to rush to my eyes. And caring not in that solitude to disguise my feelings from myself, and from the wide heaven that looked down and saw me--for this is the sweetest thing that solitude has for us, that we are free in it, and no convention holds us--I dropped on my knees and kissed the stony ground, then casting up my eyes, thanked the Author of my being for the gift of that wild forest, those green mansions where I had found so great a happiness!
— *W. H. Hudson, 1904,* Green Mansions

The cellblock unit was unusually quiet that night. The confined space where he lived like an animal in a cage held within it an escape route that he had learned to slip into without notice. He was there now, hiding within his self-contained muscular body that he had shaped with daily rigorous exercise into a threatening multi-tattooed physique. And within that hardened shell, he had discovered a new frontier that had become a revelation, a forest within his mind where he could hunt and fish and travel the woods unencumbered, tracking his way through memories of paths and trails and mountain streams where he had spent his boyhood. But there was danger even there, terrible places to avoid, memories of things never spoken, events never revealed. Thoughts were willfully pushed aside so that he could continue his exploration instead of returning to the relative safety of his cell and the prison that was less of a threat than the nightmare he would face if he lost his direction.

The Blue Ridge Mountains, part of the Appalachian Range, were also part of him, like breathing and walking and thinking. He was a creature of the forest; born, bred and raised tracking deer and bear and wild turkey. He was taught to fish and poach game at his father's knee, hunting on the vast Biltmore Estate protected forestlands that covered the mountain region adjacent to their homestead. It was a game his father had played well, often with his local politically connected cronies whom he led into the wilderness on hunting parties that sometimes turned into something else, something he didn't want to think about. But the thoughts intruded anyway, taking hold and bringing with them memories that pushed through his resistance.

He tried to flee from them back to consciousness, but they grasped his mind like it was being held in a two-handed vice and the pressure started to build. It was as if his father had him in his massive grip once more—the powerful hands and the size of the man—six foot three, and to a small boy, gigantic. The way he could turn on you in an instant, like a raging bull with cruel eyes and meanness that held no bounds. No threatening presence in his conscious existence could compare with the wrath of his father; no one. Not the major crime boss he worked for or the syndicate "made men" around him, not the ruthless gang leaders on the unit or the maniacal psychos, and no one he'd ever come across in law enforcement. No one had ever struck the fear in him that his father had, and now he was back again, invading his mind, his hunt; a dead man he could not kill.

He felt his body writhing, trying to escape the mental torment, the unbearable feeling of being trapped in it. This time he felt hopelessly caught as the memory he feared most flooded in, washing everything else away. The nightmare panic set in, producing beads of sweat on his forehead that streamed backward, dampening his hair. He felt the water swirling just beneath his head, could see the frigid current circling around him like a deadly whirlpool, and the icy fingers reaching up from the river to pull him down, down, down. His mouth opened to scream but nothing came out.

And then it happened, a miraculous soothing force pulling him away from the water, from the terror and the pain. It was a vision so pure and compelling that it drew him away from the memory with a power strange and unknown to him, leading him away from the river bank in an unfamiliar direction down a steep winding trail. The trail wound its way through a primeval forest of great majesty that opened to a beautiful cove where the water flowed gently downward from its curvature in the ridge, each side of it carpeted with brilliant shades of overhanging green foliage. Fragrant clumps of snowy white and cornflower blue wildflowers decorated the edges of the rippling stream below. He could hear the water softly rushing over pebbles and rocks and see fluid crystalline sparkles reflected in the sunlight like little beams of light floating in space. And there, reclining upon a smooth boulder of gray and white granite at the water's edge was a lovely young woman with long flaxen hair, delicate of feature and form and completely nude.

All of his senses were intensified, and yet he felt immediately soothed and comforted by her presence, and devoid of lust, despite her appearance. She looked at him, her steady gaze holding him in thrall. She was familiar, known to him, but he did not understand until she spoke. The words came to him not as a voice but as a thought in his mind. And then he knew, the knowledge wrapping his heart in a tender embrace, that she was his mother, at a time before life and hardship, before marriage and childbirth, before death had taken her to peace; when she was still innocent, a flower of the mountains, like those surrounding her.

She stared at him for a few seconds more; her eyes began to glisten and love beamed from them in streams of iridescent light. Her words came to him through his thoughts,

"You must tell the story, Bobby. This is the only thing I have ever done to help you. This will be all that I didn't do for you. Tell the story, tell it as real and true as you can, and you will be set free."

And then she disappeared and he awakened.

CHAPTER TWO

> A land of love, and a land of light,
> Without sun, or moon, or night:
> Where the river sway'd a living stream,
> And the light a pure celestial beam:
> The land of vision, it would seem
> A still and everlasting dream.
> —James Fenimore Cooper, "Queen's Wake" in *The Pathfinder*

Bobby awoke a different man, mentally transformed and physically altered by a vision of such force that he felt a molecular change in his body. He recalled hearing about such things in conversations with Jedediah Jackson, an old black inmate he'd met during his first months of incarceration. What was the word he'd used, an *epiphany*? Old Jed claimed to have had one, said that God had called him beloved, said that even his name meant "Friend of God."

"God told me so, brother. And I'd knowed it not through all those lost years."

Considering Jed's criminal history, Bobby thought something earth-shattering must have happened to make him believe that God had spoken to him, because he'd read the Bible at every opportunity and quoted the Proverbs every night in his sleep.

Bobby remembered some of them, haunting refrains of righteous words that conflicted with his daily thoughts and intentions. It irritated him like a splinter working its way inward instead of outward, an intrusion into his brain that he could not reach to extract. He'd wondered why these sayings were so vividly captured in his memory when he'd worked so hard to tune out the old man's endless ramblings.

Lately, however, Bobby had been giving them more attention, becoming curious about their meaning. Perhaps this and other recent efforts to become more spiritually grounded had opened a door in some way for the previous night's vision, a vision that remained clear and present and all around him like a protective shield. He felt warmed by it and renewed, enlightened, changed irreversibly. He was not the man he had been the day before, but was wary about disclosing what had happened and tried to act the same as always.

He sat back down on his bunk to consider the dilemma of his situation. He rarely had a moment to himself and his responsibilities were endless. Even at night, he had to keep one eye open and be hyper-vigilant, always on the alert. Sleeping was done in small doses. Perhaps that was the reason he could escape into his fantasy expeditions so easily and whenever possible. The morning ritual was about to begin and once outside their quarters, there could be no hint of the transformation he'd experienced. If word got out around the units, it might be perceived as a sign of weakness. He wanted to cry out, tell the world, and stop the menacing act but he had to stop and think instead. If he didn't, he might end up a dead man.

Fortunately for him, nothing had happened during the night to interrupt the deepest few hours of sleep he had known in years, and morning brought with it a temporary reprieve. His boss, Mickey Generoso, had been taken to the infirmary for a weekly physical awarded to no one else on the units. Not that he needed it. Approaching his eightieth birthday, he was in excellent health and well tended by his hand-picked entourage who inhabited their five-man unit cell. He was also provided with special privileges that came with his position of power; power that reached far beyond the federal institution where they were imprisoned. Bobby was an unofficial member of Mickey's crew, chosen by chance to be his personal bodyguard; a role that did not change simply because *he* had experienced a miracle.

Mickey had recently ascended from third in command within the Genovese crime family to syndicate Boss due to a decision by the overseeing Mafia Commission to replace the acting boss, Vincent (Benny the Chin) Gigante. Gigante's erratic behavior, which many believed to be an act designed to fool the FBI into thinking him mentally incompetent to stand trial, had brought embarrassment and unwanted attention to the Genovese organization. He'd feigned insanity by shuffling unshaven through New York's Greenwich Village wearing a tattered bath robe and muttering to himself incoherently. The federal indictment that eventually ensued *had* led to his confinement in a psychiatric facility instead of prison, but it resulted in the loss of his position as Boss, which he had held for years.

The fact that Mickey Generoso was in prison had made no difference to the Commission in their choice of successor. A brilliant strategist, he was not only mentally sound, he'd given a lifetime of service that commanded the respect of his peers. He was also a product of the old school in that he knew the value of discretion and the prudence of avoiding the spotlight. Unlike Gigante, Mickey embodied a quiet, steely, self-possessed reserve that held within it long-attained wisdoms handed down from centuries of mafia ritual. His benign appearance belied a fearsome reputation that inspired obedience without the use of intimidation.

His federal conviction on conspiracy charges, related to the transfer of funds obtained from stolen property, was a minor blip in an otherwise arrest-free career and the result of a snitch who had gathered evidence by infiltrating the Genovese organization. His arrest had brought about his relatively brief prison sentence at the age of seventy-seven. He'd taken his punishment with deadly calm. The snitch was placed in a witness protection program. He was "clipped" shortly thereafter, meaning that he somehow mysteriously ended up dead.

While still incarcerated, Michael "Mickey Dimino" Generoso had become head of one of the largest crime syndicates in the country; his stable of lieutenants numbered in the hundreds, ruling over a small army of soldiers. In another year, on the day of his release, a stretch limo and bodyguards would be awaiting to escort him to a private gathering where homage would be paid and his unchallenged leadership acknowledged.

The Genovese family was one of the five original Italian-American crime families that dominated organized crime in America. They originated out of already existing New York Sicilian mafia gangs. They were formally organized in the summer of 1931 by Salvatore Maranzano after the murder of Giuseppe Masseria, in what became known as the Castellammarese War. Maranzano, an admirer of the military system developed by Julius Caesar, also introduced the mafia hierarchy: Boss, Underboss, Consigliere (counselor), Capo (captain), and Soldier, and he declared himself "capo di tutti capi", the ultimate boss over all the families.

When Maranzano was murdered just months after Masseria, the "Boss of all Bosses" position was eliminated in favor of the "Commission." The Commission was a council which demarcated territory between previously warring factions and governed American mafia activities in the United States. The idea was to settle things politically amongst the families and prevent the tyranny of one man controlling all the mafia's operations. Thus, the Gambino, Genovese, Colombo, Bonanno, and Lucchese families were ruled by a higher authority made up of a group of elders who had proven their worth and wisdom and ability to outlive their enemies and rivals. The hierarchy under each Boss evolved to include Skippers, each one appointed to oversee three Captains. Each Captain had one or more Lieutenants, all of which numbered over fifty "made men" who ruled over hundreds of soldiers. These added positions aided an organization that had grown significantly since its inception.

The Genovese crime family was founded by Lucky Luciano and later named after Vito Genovese in 1957. Nicknamed the "Ivy League" and "Rolls Royce" of organized crime, they were rivaled in size by only the Gambino family and the Chicago Outfit and were unmatched in terms of power. Originally in control of the waterfront on the West Side of Manhattan (including the Fulton Fish Market), the family operated mainly in Manhattan, the Bronx, Brooklyn and New Jersey with influence in Queens, Staten Island, Long Island, Westchester County, Rockland

County, Connecticut, Massachusetts, and Florida, maintaining a varying degree of influence over many of the smaller mob families outside of New York, including ties with crime families in Buffalo, Syracuse, Albany, and Philadelphia.

Finding new ways to make money in the 21st century, the Genovese family took advantage of lax due diligence by banks during the housing spike, generating a wave of mortgage frauds. They also found ways to use new technology to improve on old reliable illegal gambling, with customers placing bets through offshore sites via the internet. And, they were one of the most difficult illegal organizations to prosecute. The family benefited like no other from members following the *Code of Omertà*.

The *Code of Omertà* arose from the Italian word *humility-modesty* and was the basis for a code of silence that was viewed as an honor code that was pledged when a soldier became a made man. During the ceremony, the image of a saint would be set alight and the inductee would state, "If I betray the oath of *Omertà*, may my soul burn in Hell like this saint." While many mobsters from across the country have testified against their crime families since the 1980s, the Genovese family has had only five of its members turn state's evidence in its history.

Mickey now ruled over this family. He had been part of the mafia world since his youth, perhaps even longer considering his hereditary influences. He was born in 1918, a second generation American of Italian immigrants (both products of Sicilian mafia families dating back generations) and raised in New York during the "Roaring Twenties." Prohibition was the law of the land then, from 1920 until 1933, and average law-abiding citizens regularly broke it by making or buying illegal liquor, some frequenting *speakeasies*, places where illegal liquor was sold. There, they mingled with an underworld society they would have otherwise completely avoided, seeking excitement that became in itself like a drug. Victorian moralities were cast asunder and gangsters rose in prominence like modern-day superstars.

A similar dichotomy occurred with Mickey during his boyhood. He was taught to be deeply religious and was indoctrinated into the ancient ritualistic Catholic religion, the faith of his parents. He was also taught other family traditions handed down by his Sicilian forefathers, and he learned how to apply them in a city that showed little mercy to the disenfranchised of its population. Immigrants helped each other by sticking with their own kind and forming groups that were made more powerful by strong allegiances. Old world customs were transposed into these organizations at the same time they were becoming more sophisticated and Americanized. Mickey graduated magna cum laude from the streets and boroughs and was accepted into one of the most powerful of all the organizations. And now, over six decades later, he had risen to the top, one of a select few.

And there was Bobby, right under his nose, chosen by him to attend to his daily needs and wishes; his faithful bodyguard who opened doors for him, carried his trays of food, protected his every move and allowed no one to touch him—even in a friendly manner—who guarded him from the slightest danger, even a slippery floor.

When the old man moved, he moved. He'd accompanied him every day on his private early morning six-mile power walks around the recreation yard, another special privilege given to Mickey purportedly for health purposes; walks that tested Bobby's endurance and caused him to wonder at the strength and resilience of the man. Bobby kept him supplied with the best food, drink, and other provisions, taking risks bartering with inmates assigned to kitchen and supply room duty, bribing to obtain goods from the outside, maneuvering within a racially and ethnically segregated territorial system of factions and gangs in order to make sure his boss was pleased and comfortable.

He deemed it an honor to fill the role he'd lived and breathed for the past two years. But even more than the responsibility and the perks that came with it, he loved the old man. Mickey had given him something he'd yearned for all his life: acceptance, praise, respect, and even a grandfatherly type of affection. At times, he'd seen a twinkle lighting the black irises in the old man's eyes—a rare event. For Bobby it was like seeing a shooting star coming straight at him out of a black night sky, and it affected him deeply because it was a sign of some deep feeling that Mickey had for him, a feeling he had somehow engendered.

Bobby liked to believe that he had sparked a glimmer of trust in Mickey, a man who trusted few due to a long past that had taught him to be suspicious and guarded. He thought maybe it was because he was not official Mafiosi: he was not one of them and could never be one of them, and therefore had no agenda or aspirations to gain something other than Mickey's genuine approval. And although he was not city-bred, nor Italian, he did live by a code borne in nature with its own unique set of principles.

Like a person from another world inserted into a clannish membership that accepted only their own kind, he was at first a mere object of interest, a temporary diversion. But Mickey had recognized in him something akin to his own talents, and from that a kinship had developed. He saw in Bobby someone who was self-governed, disciplined, a survivor—even of serious illness—with lightning quick reflexes, keen senses, and the eye of a hunter; a fellow strategist who understood human nature at its most basic level and in its most cunning and savage form.

This was the common thread that ran between them; the knowledge that, whether in a northern metropolitan city or a southern mountainous wilderness, the law of the jungle prevailed in humans as an instinctual driving force that could generate amazing feats of heroism, and in some, the foulest of deeds. To pick up on these traits in people at the earliest indication could make the difference between life and death.

Mickey was no longer the young soldier he had once been, ambitious and determined. He was no longer the made man in his prime, moving up the ranks with strategic perseverance, marking his territory along the way with threatening resolve and remarkable luck and endurance. He had reached the winter season of his life still strong for his age and had achieved, against all odds, the highest rung of power beneath the Commission. That made him a target for anyone aspiring to take his place. He had seen too many other great lions fall and hadn't forgotten the fate of Paul Castellano, who was once thought to be invincible.

Paul Constantino Castellano, also known as "the Pope", "the Howard Hughes of the Mob" and "Big Paulie", had succeeded Carlo Gambino as head of the Gambino crime family, which at that time was the nation's largest mafia family. In 1985, despite his great wealth and influential business, labor union, and political connections, he was one of many mafia bosses arrested on charges of racketeering, which was to result in the Mafia Commission Trial. In December of that year, while out on bail,

Castellano and his chauffeur and aide-de-camp, Thomas Bilotti, were shot to death outside Sparks Steak House in Manhattan on the orders of ambitious and vengeful John Gotti.

Gotti, a Gambino family 'skipper' of a large crew in Queens, the largest borough in New York, had been enraged when Castellano named Bilotti underboss instead of him. Gotti had been the protégé of the previous underboss, Aniello Delacroce, and had expected to succeed him. Castellano, convinced that Gotti could be handled and placated, had been lured to the restaurant supposedly to meet with him in order to iron out their differences. The hit team was waiting and took the unarmed Castellano and Bilotti by complete surprise, gunning them down in the street as they exited the car. Gotti and one of his crew, Sammy (the Bull) Gravano—who would later betray Gotti and testify against him—observed the hit from a car parked across the street.

Mickey had learned from experience to be overly cautious. It was not enough to have a network of protectors and an army around them. While in prison, a truce between the families existed to protect members while incarcerated. But once Mickey was released, the truce ended and he would be vulnerable. There were too many variables, as John Gotti had demonstrated. He needed a lone wolf, loyal only to him, someone he could groom for a position on the outside, someone completely trustworthy to protect him in his last days of power. Bobby embodied these traits and more. He would have laid down his life for the old man, and Mickey had come to believe it.

Bobby recalled the day they met. It was right after his first week on the unit, after he'd spent a long stretch of time moving through the convoluted hoops of the prison system to get to there. He'd been arrested and convicted on drug trafficking charges under Western North Carolina's Title: Code 18 and sentenced to six years in federal prison. The road to this final destination was a lengthy one, beginning with months in the Buncombe County Jail, followed by movement through the Federal Bureau of Prisons transfer system to a holding cell in the notorious Atlanta Penitentiary, nick-named "the Fortress", where he spent weeks before being transferred to the Kentucky Federal Medical Correctional Institution where he would spend the remainder of his sentence.

It seemed to him a twist of fate that a medical condition from which he'd completely recovered had proved beneficial by bringing him to this facility. After his arrest, when his lawyer, Sean Devereux, learned that he'd years before been diagnosed and treated for Stage-4 Hodgkin's Lymphoma, once called Hodgkin's disease, he'd been able to use that information to direct the course of his confinement. Although Bobby had been successfully treated and was in the best physical condition of his life, Hodgkin's was considered a potentially chronic condition. As a result, after processing, he'd been transported to the same institution where Mickey Generoso resided, primarily because of his advanced age.

The Kentucky facility was old; it dated back to the 1930s when it had been a Federal Narcotics Farm. Its original purpose was to house people who were admitted voluntarily with drug abuse problems and treat them, with mostly experimental treatments; it was the first of its kind in the United States. In 1974, the institution became a federal medical correctional prison but maintained a "psychiatric hospital" title until 1998, when two inmates killed another inmate with a fire extinguisher. Although the population didn't change, the psychiatric hospital was assimilated into the correctional system.

The prison was surrounded by two 12-foot fences with a 45-degree angle roll of tangled razor-wire at the top, electronically monitored and extensively guarded. New prisoners were processed in the large main building which had a series of entry checkpoints eventually leading to a wing that housed an open dorm-style unit with forty beds and foot lockers to store personal items. This was another temporary holding area nicknamed "the bus stop" where another two or three weeks could pass before one was assigned a housing unit.

The first days in a federal institution of any kind could be precarious. Bobby approached the situation as if he were entering an untamed forest. He observed everything around him from the entry point to the internal structure of the facility. He took in every key factor related to his location, inscribing in his memory every detail as he was led through the corridors toward his assigned bed and locker. He picked up on every movement, every action, voice, attitude, and any indication of threat. For the first week, he held his breath while assessing his level of danger in the scheme of things, trying to get "the lay of the land." After two and a half weeks, he was assigned to a unit.

The Antaeus Unit was located on the west wing of the institution and housed both the general population and those needing a minimal level of medical care. The physical layout of the unit housing area included three floors consisting of three dormitories and a configuration of cell-rooms that ran along cell-block hallways that extended from corridors connected to a central dormitory area. Each cell room could house up to five inmates. The general administrative staff and guard offices ran along a staff alley located on the first floor of the unit, monitoring all access to and from the upper floors.

Each corridor represented a section and branched off from a central dormitory which represented a unit. A guard was assigned to each section in a constant rotation of shifts, a unit manager to each unit. While the set-up in the medical institution was less confining than most prison settings, it was still a prison, and his new room was still a cell he had to share with strangers. So he maintained his reserve and kept to himself, at the same time searching for a familiar face during recreation period in the yard. It wasn't long before he recognized someone with whom he'd had previous dealings.

Before his arrest, he'd made associations with wise guys from the North, supplying them with illegal products sent up the pipeline that linked Western North Carolina to Philadelphia. One of them, a crew member of the Gambino family by the name of Dominick Marcuso, was also assigned to the Antaeus Unit. Once a day, inmates were given a recreation period in the lower courtyard referred to as "the yard." It was there that Bobby made contact with Dominick and was greatly relieved when he remembered him. They only had a few brief conversations, but each one was noticed and helped to deflect unwanted interest from gang faction members that hung out together around the yard.

It was obvious to Bobby that Dominick carried some heavy weight, and so did the two guys he hung out with, because they had prime territory in the yard and no one dared to intrude upon it, even though they were a small group of three. Dominick finally introduced Bobby to them, but this did not guarantee his acceptance by this trio made up of Dominick, Rick Fusco, a Colombo family captain, and Johnny Gammarano, a Gambino "made man" known as Johnny G. Johnny G shared a cell-room with Dominick and another man who was not in the yard that day, a man whom they talked about in silent whispers.

Bobby was impressed with the fact that this group was made up of men from different mob affiliations. He learned from Dominick that it was a mafia commission expectation that divergent mafia family members band together when in prison and form a truce until their release. There was also a ban on hits ordered from the outside. This expectation was taken as a rule, and although there had been infractions in some prisons over the years, particularly during times of heated mob warfare, the truce was for the most part respected and adhered to. Bobby also felt grateful to Dominick for telling Johnny G and Richie Fusco about his mob connections in Philly, and his fearsome reputation, which helped to establish some level of respect and a certain amount of inclusion, at least when they were out in the yard. Unfortunately, his new acquaintances could not help him avoid the next situation he faced, which took place indoors when he had gotten misdirected returning from the Central Clinic and found himself in the wrong place at the wrong time.

Each unit had a schedule that ran like clockwork. Guards were on eight hour rotation and call down was done at 4:00 p.m. each day for a head count and inspection. The inspection rating applied to the condition of each unit and the timely completion of jobs that were assigned. When one unit was slack, by even one performance of duty, all the residents on that unit suffered the loss of privileges, like going to meals on time. The residents on the unit that received the highest inspection rating were the first in line for meals and recreation time. All privileges had great meaning in this setting, and going last or loss of a single one was a punishing experience. Therefore, completion of every job was important; even mopping the floor was a big deal.

In the second week of residence, during the recreation period, Bobby was excused for an initial health screening at the Central Clinic, a restricted access area that was otherwise considered out of bounds unless a pass was issued. After the examination, he was led back to the west wing by a guard and then released into the locked-in unit where he was able to return alone down a long corridor that led to his section. The unit guard on duty was nowhere to be seen and he turned down a hallway that he mistook for the one leading to his room. Eyes cast downward and lost in his thoughts, wondering if his screening would prove him to be as healthy as he felt, he didn't realize until it was too late that he was walking down the wrong hallway on a soaking wet floor.

He was just about to turn around and head back when he saw the 360-pound frame of a massive inmate named Johnny Johnson steamrolling toward him from the other end of the hallway. He'd apparently been using the recreation period to finish up his hall duty. Bobby put his hands up in a gesture of apology and backtracked along the edge of the floor, trying not to leave footprints. His efforts were in vain. Any mark on the floor was cause for demerit and Johnson had a reputation for being a stark raving maniac.

Bobby's physique was strong and muscular and he was an expert in jujitsu. But Johnson towered over him in size and was coming toward him fast, his face constricted with rage, his eyes glaring with menace, and his mouth spewing a stream of obscenities that rose in timber from a guttural growl to a thunderous roar.

"What the hell are you doin' walking on my floor. I'm going to kick the shit out of you and use you to mop it up."

Bobby tried to keep his cool and said, "You don't have to lay a foul tongue on me," a mountain expression that Johnson couldn't comprehend.

Johnson continued to bear down on him like a human freight train, but made the mistake of taking the time to say,

"What the fuck are you sayin', you worthless redneck hillbilly bastard. I'll kill you before you can spit. I'll grind you up into . . ."

A door opened several yards down the hallway in response to Johnson's loud voice. Moving from inside to outside the doorway, two witnesses watched with interest as Bobby interrupted his formidable opponent mid-threat with a lightning fast right-hand fist that landed in the hollow of Johnson's left eye, followed in quick succession by a left-hand strike that centered on John-son's protuberant chin. Johnson staggered backward and then leaned forward in a rocking unbalanced motion and then col-lapsed with a heavy thud onto the shiny wet floor.

Bobby stood over the unconscious mountainous heap and said without triumph, "Knocked out cold by a 200-pound hill-billy redneck."

He hadn't realized he was overheard and was startled to hear the sound of quiet laughter coming from down the hallway. He turned to his left, and with some distance between them, faced an elderly man he did not recognize who stood next to a taller dark-haired one he immediately recognized as Johnny G. They had also apparently not been required to join the others in the courtyard; he had never seen the much older man there. Much to Bobby's relief, the man smiled slightly and nodded to Johnny G, who then looked at Bobby and said, "Come on in, kid."

With some reluctance, he accepted the invitation into the room, even though he had only a few minutes before he would be due back in his section before the others returned. When he entered, he was surprised by the difference between the interior of the room from his own cell-room. It looked the same size, but was set up more like an apartment, with kitchen appliances and a microwave, a dining table, and comfortable chairs. There was enough space to accommodate five residents but it appeared that only three lived there, and the elder man's bed was sectioned off from the rest.

There was no doubt in Bobby's mind about the identity of the old man. He had heard enough from Dominick to know that he was about to be introduced to Mickey Generoso, newly ap-pointed Boss of the Genovese family. He was at a loss for words until the darkly handsome Johnny G introduced him to Mickey. Bobby was instructed to address him as Mickey rather than the more reverent Mr. Generoso. His position as Boss was never to be acknowledged in front of others and he was to be referred to as "just one of the guys." This was of course ludicrous because his power was absolute and everyone around him knew it.

Mickey's presence was palpable; Bobby could feel it but could not pinpoint a physical characteristic that explained it. He was only about five foot eight or nine inches in height, his build slight, almost wispy, but he appeared to be fit, trim and wiry. His movements were quick but graceful, his hair thick and combed straight back. His grooming was fastidious, his expression stern, giving the impression of stoicism. And then Bobby saw it—it was in his eyes—large black pools behind glasses that rested on his prominent nose. There was a glint in the irises that could turn soft or steely in a second, and it happened several times in turn while he was standing there in front of the man. In one instant he'd felt a chill.

Bobby felt almost giddy, having emerged intact from his skirmish with Johnson only to find himself face to face with a major syndicate mob boss. He tried to be polite, respectful, even congenial, in a mountain friendly way that self-consciously erupted from sheer nervousness. He felt caught like a deer in the headlights and knew what a vulnerable position that was. He was soon relieved to learn that his exploit with Johnson had provided Mickey with the best entertainment he'd had in months.

"You got a hell of a right, kid, and you're quick on your feet. You'd be handy to have around. What do you think, G?"

Johnny G looked at the old man thoughtfully. Bobby watched him think about it for a few seconds and worried that he might have some objection. In those seconds, old Jed's voice popped into Bobby's mind, quoting the old Hebrew saying,

"It is impossible for God to lie."

Translated to fit this situation, Bobby took it to mean, "Whatever Mickey says is the truth."

Then he knew that there would be no disagreement from Johnny G, it just wasn't possible. Johnny nodded his head in agreement and his thoughts remained silent.

After a brief questioning period during which Mickey listened intently, Bobby gave them a truthful account of his past activities that led him to being entrapped and arrested by the feds. He described his special skills and connections, some of his family history, and told them his street name, Bo, and the reason he'd garnered the nicknames Bo-guns, Bo-blades, and Bo-diesel. Mickey almost laughed at that point and his eyes reflected his amusement. Bobby instinctively knew in that moment, his Southern sensibilities alerted, that Mickey was not silently laughing at him, which would have been hard to take, but was instead quietly enjoying something about him. For a young man seeking the slightest sign of approval from an older, respected authority figure and having received both praise for his actions and a gesture of genuine acceptance, it was like a door opening to all the need inside of him that was yearning to be fulfilled. There would be no question about where his loyalty would be placed and he and Mickey knew it before he was unceremoniously excused.

When the door closed behind him, the hallway stretched out long and empty toward the main corridor. There was no sign of Johnson and the floor was dry and polished. When he made it back to his room, there were no remarks from his cell-mates or repercussions for his absence. The guard on duty did stare at him for a prolonged, unsettling moment during call-down inspection but said nothing. The rest of the day and night proceeded as usual. The next morning, he was awakened by the same guard and told to gather his belongings. He did as he was told and then followed him as instructed to the hallway where Mickey resided. He gave no explanation until they reached the door and then said,

"Well, you're in with the mob now."

And then he turned and walked away. Bobby watched him with curiosity until he was out of sight, only then quietly expressing his thoughts, "Yeah, you probably think I'm in league with the devil."

But then he figured the guard had to be on the take to have brought him there and that they were both in the same league. Only in Bobby's mind, it was more like being in league with a god than a devil. The boss of a mob family was the closest thing to a god that Bobby could think of. He didn't think of it as being sacrilegious. It was just the way it was—like it was when he was a child.

He'd been taught by his mother and grandparents to pray to the true God and try to be a good boy in His eyes. They taught him to believe that God was always watching. But his father ruled his life and there was no escaping it, despite his prayers. It had been impossible to be a good boy while under his father's thumb. He would have been squashed like an ant. So he'd tried to pretend that God wasn't looking at him, or couldn't see him, in an effort to hide the bad things from God's eyes. And later he tried to believe that God wasn't there at all. But always there remained a part of him that believed that God existed. He just couldn't believe that God existed for him.

CHAPTER THREE

As my grandmother bent over me to brush and straighten my clothes, she always said the same thing. 'Like a Mongolian,' she sighed. 'Just like a little Mongolian.' I never heard anyone else speak of the mysterious Mongolians, and I had no idea who they were. I recognized the word was an admonition of sorts but I sensed it also contained a note of praise. I liked its unruliness and its ambiguities, and I wanted to live up to the idea of recklessness that it seemed to imply. Long before I had any clear sense of Mongolia as a place, the word belonged to those intense adventures played out each evening in the slow descent of an Irish twilight, as I tugged against the mooring of my grandmother's voice calling me home.
—Stanley Stewart, who grew up to author
In the Empire of Genghis Khan

"Bobby, you come home now," she called from the front porch into the high winds that carried her voice across the ridge. "That youngin'," she said to herself and shook her head, "he'd be running wild like a Cherokee renegade from morning until night if I let him."

He heard his grandmother's voice and tried to ignore her call. He'd been working on a hole covered with a stick branch pile as delicately woven and intricate as a beaver dam; he'd constructed a turkey trap and then covered with a thin layer of leaves. He'd heard the gobblers on the ridge the day before and found their tracks and knew where they'd be crossing. He'd catch one for sure and take it to her, and she'd look at him with surprise and pretend to fuss, but he'd see her eyes get all shiny and dewy and he'd know that she was pleased with him. After the gobbler would be put to its end, they'd sit on the porch and pluck its feathers while water was put on to boil in the kitchen. And then before dinner, she'd make those big fluffy biscuits and maybe a cobbler and there'd be a special blessing said to thank the good Lord for the food — even though *He* hadn't caught the turkey. But that'd be okay, because that's the way his grandmother saw things, and he guessed that maybe the Lord had something to do with that turkey being there, too.

His Grandma Stanton was soft and smooth, womanly, he thought, and always talking about the good Lord and taking him to church to hear preaching whenever he stayed with her and grandpa. They were a loving pair, devoted to one another and to him. His grandfather was an educated man, a retired lawyer who loved to play chess and read Shakespeare. He doted on his wife, often praising her for her beauty — "ageless," he would say. It was peaceful there and Bobby wished he could stay with them all the time. He was never afraid there, not even when his grand-mother was calling him home after he'd stayed out too long. Her will was strong, but it was her love that called to him and reached into his heart. It was the irresistible force that broke down his resistance.

He'd asked her one time why she was always calling him a Cherokee renegade and she'd explained, "Because you run through the woods like a wild Indian, but not just any Indian. The Cherokees were hard to get out of these forests, honey, and born to it just like you. The ones that rebelled against being tak-en out didn't get sent far away to the state of Oklahoma like the others. There was one Eastern band of them that ended up being able to stay on their native land not far from here, up towards Tennessee where the forest land around that area is just as pret-ty as here. So when I call you a renegade, it's not always a bad thing; sometimes being a rebel is good, as long as it's for a good reason, and if it's done with a noble heart. And I know you have one because of all the brave and lovin' things you do for me."

So he never again minded when she called him that.

Grandma and Grandpa Stanton were his mother's parents. They lived across the mountains from the home where he lived by the French Broad River. The west and east sides of that part of the mountain chain were worlds apart in Bobby's mind, as different as darkness and light. At home, he'd grow fearful when the sun dipped below the face of the mountain and turned it black. It was like someone had reached up and pulled down a nightshade of gloom on the spirit. But even so, he was pulled to the dark side of the mountain by his father's will just as powerfully as he was drawn to the benevolent light that seemed to emanate from his grandmother's beckoning call.

The differences in that seven mile span that separated Bobby's mother from her parents were not unlike the mountainous region where they lived and encompassed the same paradoxes found in some of its people. From earliest time, the mountains that surrounded them had evolved from chaos and eruption into a landscape that seemed touched by a creator of profound artistic mastery. The Natives and early explorers alike were encircled within its captivating embrace and held there by the promise of independence and freedom.

The French Broad River near his home sprang from the ancient mountain slopes that were part of the Appalachian range extending from northern Alabama to Canada, the oldest mountains in North America, created long before the Rocky Mountains. A product of nature's violence, through mighty earthquakes and colossal upheavals, they formed over the centuries into majestic peaks of startling beauty. The spectacular Blue Ridge Mountain chain that divided North Carolina and Tennessee enclosed a plateau area of approximately six thousand square miles, the culminating region of the Appalachian system, which contained not only its largest masses but its highest summits, the highest east of the Mississippi River. The chain was divided by many cross ridges into a number of smaller plateaus and basins, each bounded on all sides by high mountains sheltering corresponding rivers and valleys, all arranged with a rare combination of order and symmetry.

A few miles northeast of the city of Asheville, a single short ridge known as the Black Mountains extended in a northerly direction from the Blue Ridge chain. Its total length was about fifteen miles, but within this short distance a dozen peaks rose to an elevation of more than six thousand feet above sea level, the highest being Mt. Mitchell.

From some of these mountainsides a forest extended north for more than a thousand miles, encompassing a variety of trees richer than all of Europe: stands of virgin spruce and balsam fir, primeval pine and poplar, walnut, oak, hickory, chestnut, and maple. The cold rippling springs that fed thousands of steady streams created the giant French Broad River, the heart and the blood of the forest. Valleys formed by the mountain streams flowed deep and narrow, spurting a multitude of cascading waterfalls, some of amazing height and velocity. During spring and summertime, plants and shrubs and wildflowers erupted in an explosion of color; flaming wood azaleas burned orange and crimson, rhododendrons bloomed in shades of pink and lavender and intertwined with mountain laurel bushes that blanketed the slopes in glorious soft pink profusion and belied their treacherous interwoven entanglements.

In the forests of the French Broad, insects unique to the area flourished in hollow trees and rotting logs. Rock slides and springs provided habitats for rare specimens of wildlife and plant-life that brought scientists from all over the world to study their varieties. And the mountain people, too, were as rare in quality as the plants and creatures that inhabited this wilderness. They were as varied and resilient, complex and adaptable, and bound to nature as their life blood and spiritual center.

During the middle of the eighteenth century, the first settlers came from the Virginia, Pennsylvania, Maryland, and New Jersey regions, migrating westward and southwestward. They crossed the Blue Ridge Mountain barrier into the high western North Carolina Plateau and traveled downward through the gaps and the watersheds into the valley of the French Broad and the land of the Cherokees. They were Scotch–Irish, English, French Huguenot, Dutch and German pioneers. Others came later from the Eastern coast, the Scotch–Irish predominating and infusing their heritage into the region. Whether escaping famine, oppression, taxation, or threat of imprisonment for debt, they were driven by determination, unyielding individualism, and a desire for independence, and they were willing to brave a primordial wilderness to find it.

In the beginning, they traded with the Cherokees and bartered for land with rich soil, plentiful wood and water, and good hunting grounds. It was a bountiful land, as luxuriant and green as the fresh rolling hills and dales of Ireland, with misty mountains as tree-covered and dense as the mystic highlands of Scotland. They were hunters and explorers, fishermen, ranchers, farmers, traders and merchants. They felled the timber and built cabins and settlements in isolated areas and along the French Broad River where trade transformed wilderness into small communities, like the settlement village that was to later become the city of Asheville.

Land grants and settlement brought with them land encroachment and brutal skirmishes with the Cherokees, a people with whom they had initially intermingled and befriended. Pacts were broken, the rationalization being that the land was meant to be settled and planted and harvested by white civilized people. This sense of entitlement led to years of battle and massacre on both sides and the eventual decimation of the Cherokee nation in 1776. After their defeat, an agreement was made between North Carolina and the Cherokee nation chiefs to purchase from them the French Broad territory that would later become Buncombe County, where the village of Asheville was located. Civil War followed, loyalties were bitterly divided, and despite the horrific death and destruction that ensued, the pioneers of the French Broad remained entrenched in a land that was often as harsh as the enemies they fought to keep it.

These early pioneers were strong-willed and industrious. They had to be, for despite their progress and acquisitions they were isolated by colossal natural boundaries and cut off from the mainstream of a growing new post-Revolutionary War nation. They made their own farming equipment, furniture, and almost everything else they used. They made what they didn't have and could not buy. They raised their own food, sheared and spun wool for clothes, and forged iron into tools, knives, and horseshoes. They built saw mills and tanneries, and water-powered grist mills for grinding corn, a staple of life in the mountains, just as firearms were essential to survival.

Rifle-guns were made by men who became renowned for creating weapons of precision and accuracy. Marksmanship was valued above all and shooting-match competitions were held to prove who was champion of the mountains. It was more than an effort to outdo one another. These were stoic self-reliant men who ventured into the tangled depths of the forest and climbed up steep and rugged terrains to hunt in territory that required them to have an instinct for survival and an ability to use their weapons with exceptional skill. All seasons were hunting seasons and a hunter's limit was how much he could bag and carry home.

From morning to night in autumn, a hunter could shoot enough bears to provide his family with bear-bacon for the winter months and skins for trade at market. Typically clad in buckskin, he hunted through the gaps and hollows and ridges where smooth-running streams could become treacherous waterfalls hidden by thick mazes of twisted laurel and interlocking vines. He plunged through bramble thickets and underbrush, climbing the rocky ridges upward to summits and peaks that overlooked vast acres of un-tracked forest. In some areas, well-worn Indian trails presented another form of danger, the possibility of ambush, the potential for an attack. And on he would trek through streams and gorges where gigantic boulders could dislodge and slide and crush a man in an instant.

Wild turkeys were easy prey and there were beaver, otter, muskrat, squirrel, fox, coon, groundhog, deer, pheasant and quail. The wild game was plentiful. But hunters had to have a keen understanding of their prey and stalked it in areas inhabited by black bear and panthers, wolves, cougar and bobcats: predators that could tear a man to shreds in seconds.

The hunters either knew each other or knew of each other and formed a method of connection through marked trail signals and trading post word-of-mouth communication that few on the outside could understand. Rawboned and daring, they thrived in the most isolated conditions and challenged prodigious natural barriers and obstacles in exchange for their freedom and independence. They were backwoodsmen who lived on the fringe of the wilderness and were territorial, fierce in rivalry, deadly marksmen, and rugged individualists. And when they settled, they settled in family clans that were like small communities inviting no interference unless it was welcomed. Loyalties and hatreds ran deep and family lines carried on this tradition. Churches were built and many attended; the Bible was the bedrock and often quoted, but the mountain code that developed alongside it was spoken in secret and was as moral and immoral as a two-sided coin.

For over a hundred years after the first settlements, there existed a way of life governed by rules, laws, and a sense of justice that grew in isolation while a United States and a federal government formed around them and concentrated on areas outside of this region. The people were protected by an Appalachian range that made intrusion into their lives nearly impossible. Initial attempts to open the area to the rest of the world were met with a multitude of setbacks and failures. When water travel was tried on the French Broad, the river destroyed most of the first riverboats and early experiments to turn it into a workable waterway. The railroad companies were defeated again and again during a long series of conflicts and disasters, man-made and natural, which thwarted every effort to lay the iron track into the upper French Broad valley. Politicians, swindlers, war, poverty, pneumonia, granite rock and mudslides were only a few of the problems that prevented progress — until 1875, when an act of the North Carolina Legislature provided that:

> The Warden of the Penitentiary shall, from time to time, as the Governor may direct, send to the President of said company all convicts who have not been farmed out...to labor on said railroad, provided the convicts assigned shall be at least five hundred and the number so assigned shall not exceed five hundred.

With the State of North Carolina furnishing the labor needed to finish the railroads across the mountains to Asheville, the largest obstacle facing any railroad builder, the grade on the eastern slope of the Blue Ridge, was completed. This work was done by hand and sweat and blood using pick and shovel, carts and mules, axes and saws and hand drilling of rock. Even the dynamite was homemade. The engineers and convicts working together bored and blasted up the steep ascent of 1100 vertical feet, looping up the mountain by curving back and forth stretching the treacherous three impossible miles into seven and one half miles of workable track. During the heaviest construction there were 1455 men and boys laboring to clear the path and over a thousand mules, horses and oxen. No one ever revealed or estimated the number of graves that were left in the wake of an undertaking that would change the lives and destiny of the people of the French Broad. At its completion, the Western North Carolina line was considered the marvel of railroad engineering in the United States and hailed as a scenic wonder that captured the interest of travelers worldwide.

When the railroad came, so did industry, timber companies and land speculators, and an outside civilization and upper crust society that completely underestimated the people they encountered. Businessmen, travelers, wealthy and educated people from elsewhere did not always recognize the natural intelligence the mountain people possessed or the richness of the culture. Their language and customs seemed backward, and lack of formal education in many cases was mistaken for ignorance. Their humble dwellings and way of life were a distinct contrast from the luxurious homes, attire, and customs of the class conscious newcomers.

But they were not too ignorant to take advantage of the opportunities afforded by the jobs that were created, opportunities that had been previously unknown. And it was soon discovered by company bosses and wealthy landowners that the mountain people of this region had a level of self-respect that could not be diminished by any man. They were not impressed by the values of outsiders and instead stood on an equal ground with them.

The independent spirit that was characteristic of the early frontiersmen and settlers had been fostered by its people in a land that demanded it for their survival. By sheer inventiveness and determination, they had become one with a wilderness that was now being discovered anew by a society that rode trains and fine carriages and thought themselves to be better. But this was the land that bred such men as Davey Crockett. The newcomers would eventually learn that there was much more to these mountain-folk than met the eye.

From necessity and industry there had developed over time a culture of men and women proficient in numerous areas. It was

not unusual for one person to master numerous skills and occupations. A proprietor of a tavern could also be a hotel-keep-
er, run a blacksmith shop, be the local postmaster, and owner
of a mill. A storekeeper could also be a carpenter, shoemaker,
painter, plumber, harness and saddle-maker, and candle-maker.
A farmer could be a hunter, bee-raiser, butcher, fruit-grower,
poulterer, gardener, Bible scholar, and run a stable, and a physician could also be lawyer, politician, and school master. A pillar
of the church could also have a large extended family infiltrated
into every area of business and local politics, strategically positioned to influence county judicial affairs in his favor. It was
a homespun network as intricate and as complex as the inter-
workings of a beehive.

This interweaving of talents and occupations included the
unreported practice of bartering and the unregulated making
and selling of corn liquor, practices that were considered a form
of tax evasion by federal law enforcement authorities who were
beginning to take an interest now that they had greater access to
the area. But whiskey making and bartering continued despite
efforts to enforce laws related to these practices. The mountain
people responded to this intrusion the same way they responded
to the new society that was trying to change their way of life.
On the surface it appeared that a mutual interdependence had
developed between the old and the new, and communities were
prospering as a result. Beneath the surface, the old ways continued and the mountain code expanded to include methods of
resistance to restrictions and taxations, and enforcement of the
law in relation to these impositions was met with a secretive
underground practice of lawbreaking.

It was during this period, in 1888, that a member of America's
reigning aristocracy, George Washington Vanderbilt III, grandson of shipping and railroading magnate Cornelius Vanderbilt,
visited the growing city of Asheville on a trip with his mother.
They stayed in a fashionable old hotel atop a hill at the edge of
town. After settling in, he walked out onto the wide hotel ve-
randa and was completely awestruck by the view. From his elevated vantage point, he could see the winding French Broad
River and the lush forestland beyond that rose in the distance to
mountain ridges of spellbinding beauty, their misty blue peaks

dominated by the towering Mount Pisgah. It seemed a land from another time, untamed and glorious. A young man of sensitive nature who began collecting books, antiques, and paintings at an early age, he became enthralled with the spectacle before him. Not only were his artistic imagination sparked and his visionary spirit inflamed — like the adventurers who came before him, he felt compelled to become a part of it.

Shortly thereafter he came into an inheritance of great wealth. With his dream still alive, he returned to Asheville and began purchasing land that would eventually total 125,000 acres. Two years later, construction began on the site he had previously viewed from the hotel. For the next five years, from 1890 until 1895, on a plateau rising gently from the upper French Broad River, he built a French Renaissance-style chateau that would become the largest, most distinctive home in the United States.

Vanderbilt not only employed thousands of workers, he chose the most skilled architect, landscape gardener, and sculptor he could find, along with stonecutters, carpenters and artisans imported from other countries. Local labor was hired and trained to build and landscape a home that he would name Biltmore House, derived from "Bildt", the region in Holland where the Vanderbilt family originated, and the old English word for "rolling upland country." When completed, the mansion would house 255 rooms sitting on a five-acre foundation. It was like a castle being built in a feudal kingdom where the people who lived there had never before experienced anything like it or seen so much wealth represented. The Biltmore estate changed the landscape dramatically and also became an intrinsic part of it, as he had wished.

George Vanderbilt's home was finished but his life was not complete. After another year of overseeing finishing touches on the estate, he left for a trip to Europe. There, he met and fell in love with Edith Stuyvesant Dresser, who after a brief courtship accepted his proposal of marriage. They were married in Paris in June of 1898 and no bride could have come home to a more unique and beautiful place to begin her married life. Their first and only child, Cornelia, was born two years later at the turn of the century.

Outside the great iron gates of the estate entrance, a model village was built, patterned after an English squire's village, complete with church, school and hospital. The adjacent city of Asheville began to flourish with fresh produce, dairy and meat from the Biltmore Estate dairy and greenhouses. Art and handicraft industries were born due to the encouragement and support of Edith Vanderbilt, and the city attracted a social climbing aristocracy that provided a court for the modest industrious king Vanderbilt and his wife and child.

Vanderbilt loved being surrounded by his family and friends but was more concerned with developing his ideal environment than entertaining society. The 200 acres immediately surrounding the estate had been turned into a magnificent formal landscape and gardens. He then turned his efforts toward the Mt. Pisgah section of the forest that had inspired him to live there. Many of the woodlands east of the French Broad River had been recklessly cut and burned over the years. Thousands of acres of abandoned clearings and erosion had already begun to scar the fields and hillsides. He employed Gifford Pinchot, who became the first trained forester in America, to develop the first comprehensive forest plan in the Western Hemisphere and renovation began on this area.

He then brought in Dr. Carl A. Schenck from Darmstadt, Germany, who had impressed him with work he had done in Germany's famous Black Forest. Schenck was appointed Chief Forester, and under Vanderbilt's sponsorship founded the Biltmore School of Forestry in 1898, the first in America. Under Schenck's supervision, work began on large tracts of Mt. Pisgah woodland, west of the river where the forest was much denser and appeared wildly unmanageable. There, the new innovation of selective cutting was introduced. Logging roads were laid out with such ingenious planning that they later became permanent mountain roads. The first foresters were trained, and management and conservation began using forestry science practices that had been established in France and Germany.

Wildlife was studied, identified, cataloged, and protected as never before. Predatory bobcat, coyote, fox, and red wolves stalked their prey. Muskrat, otter, opossum, weasel, groundhog, squirrel and shrew followed their wily routines, beaver built their dams in architectural delight, wild turkey, deer and elk stayed ever on the alert, and long-nosed pigs rooted for acorns. Wild geese flew over the lakes and streams, varieties of ducks, ring-necked pheasants, guinea hens, and grouse decorated the meadows and ponds, and the black bear reigned supreme. It was a Garden of Eden, lush and abundant, with a treasure trove of game.

It was a poacher's dream.

And only one-half mile up the French Broad River from the sprawling Biltmore estate, lived the family into which Bobby's father was born. To understand him, one must understand everything that came before him, the mountain people who raised him, and the forest land that he would come to believe was his birthright.

CHAPTER FOUR

As I came home through the woods with my string of fish, trail-
ing my pole, it being now quite dark, I caught a glimpse of a woodchuck
stealing across my path, and felt a strange thrill of savage delight, and
was strangely tempted to seize and devour him raw; not that I was hun-
gry then, except for that wildness which he represented. Once or twice,
however, while I lived at the pond, I found myself ranging the woods, like
a half-starved hound, with strange abandonment, seeking some kind of
venison which I might devour, and no morsel could have been too savage
for me. The wildest scenes had become unaccountably familiar. I found
in myself, and still find, an instinct toward a higher, or, as it is named,
spiritual life, as do most men, and another toward a primitive, rank, and
savage one, and I reverence them both.
— *H.D. Thoreau*, Walden: Or Life in the Woods

They named him Robert. He was the fourth child and the
baby of the family. There would be no more children to follow,
and so he was doted upon. He was the *leastin*, the Celtic word for
"the last one," a role as significant as eldest son but with far less
responsibility.

Their land was situated up the French Broad River about a
quarter of a mile from the Biltmore Estate boundary line. Their
homestead sat farther back because of the river's curve inward
but it was also closer in vicinity to Asheville, on the western side

of the city. By the time of Robert's birth, the first two decades of the twentieth century had passed, along with the glory days of the Biltmore Estate. George Vanderbilt's great wealth and vision had transposed a dream into reality, but his untimely death in 1914 brought unexpected changes to the estate. During the following decade, his widow Edith deeded a large portion of it to the United States forming the Pisgah National Forest; 8,000 acres remained part of the estate.

Robert was born in 1924, the same year that George and Edith's only child, Cornelia Vanderbilt, married The Honorable John Francis Amherst Cecil, third son of Lord William Cecil, the Marques of Exeter, a direct descendent of William Cecil, Lord Burghley and High Treasurer to Queen Elizabeth the First. This melding of European and American society had only increased the American fascination with royalty, despite the war for independence that had been won against monarch rule. However, the great extravagances that existed among this social class created a wide chasm of separation between the rich and the poor.

Unlike Europe, America's "royalty" was for the most part a product of the Industrial Revolution which had transformed the workforce of the country. The French Broad region and the city of Asheville had been transformed by the Vanderbilts, along with timber and industrial barons who had also been drawn to the area, but none of it would have happened without the railroad. Robert's father was a railroad engineer.

Typical of the mountain culture, he was also a man of many abilities and trades, and one of them was bootlegging illegally distilled corn whiskey. It was a family operation that had started long before the railroads came and would continue throughout times of prosperity and recession. It was the reason the family had a sizable rambling home that also served as a boarding house, and it had kept them from being as poverty stricken as many were during that time. And business was good, primarily due to passage of the Volstead Act, which was the 18th Amendment to the Constitution. Prohibition—later seen as exemplary of "the law of unintended consequences"—had become the law of the land. But the making of home-made whiskey pre-dated Prohibition; it was a centuries-old tradition, mastered by the Scotch-Irish.

The process of converting corn crops into whiskey began as an effort to simplify transport for the sale of corn outside the region. The roads throughout the Blue Ridge and Appalachian Plateau were rough and the high cost of construction prevented improvements. Farmers who grew more than enough corn to feed their families and livestock often could not afford to transport the surplus to market. Once the bulky corn was concentrated into liquor, however, farmers could transport it more easily and still make a profit, unless they were taxed too heavily.

To avoid this taxation, illegal distilleries, "stills," became a concentrated home industry in rural mountain counties. The liquor was also not taxed when transported and sold illegally and was profitable because it competed with legal products that were more expensive to purchase. Distribution was not limited to local customers and vicinities. Unlicensed bars called "nip joints" were located in many urban areas and a supply connection to these operations increased profits. It wasn't that illegal liquor couldn't be made in the cities. The problem was that the distillation process required substantial heat to boil the mash and separate the alcohol vapor from the water vapor. Mountaineers could use wood, whereas city moonshiners would have to use electricity or gas, making the process more expensive and easier to detect. When Prohibition became law, demand for illegal moonshine skyrocketed, the legal competition was removed, and a new form of law enforcement was introduced.

Whiskey made in stills was called "moonshine" because it was made at night in the moonlight to hide the smoke from informers and tax agents, called revenuers. The moonshiners worked in hollows and coves and above river streams, backwoods areas that provided water and tangled ridges that provided camouflage. Traditionally, moonshiners sold by trusted word-of-mouth and in their local area. Their customers had to seek them out and look in the right places, have the right contacts, and be sworn to secrecy. There were code words they used to talk to each other about the business. This secret language was used to protect them from the law. Names for moonshine included white lightning, skull cracker, rotgut, mule kick, hillbilly pop, panther's breath, cool water, old horsey, bush whiskey, and sweet spirits of cats a-fighting. The moonshiner made the whiskey and the bootleggers sold and distributed it.

It was a systematic network that operated to keep the liquor flowing and moving. The bootleggers, who set up distribution points and organized runners to take the product to buyers, were part of an underground web of participants; some of them were friends and neighbors, some were pillars of the community, and some ran legal or illegal businesses. Distribution points were trusted places where contacts were made and some of the contraband was stored until it could be safely moved.

Once moonshine started selling on a larger scale, delivering it created an industry of its own. Although the term "bootlegging" had been around since Colonial days—colonists were discouraged from selling liquor to Native Americans but continued to sell it or use it in trade by hiding it in the top of their boot, covered by the pant leg—the bootleggers of the 1920s and 30s brought new meaning to the word.

Bootleggers of this era devised a number of ways to avoid capture while transporting the liquor. One of the most common ways was to "soup up" the engines of the cars they drove. They were renegades of the road, racing vehicles at top speed, avoiding obstacles at every turn, and maneuvering around dangerous blind curves and narrow snake-like roads with fearless audacity. They honed their driving skills by competing with each other in back road races, playing cops and robbers in reckless cat-and-mouse chases with their cars and trucks. Mechanics who worked on these vehicles became masters of the art and were renowned for their abilities. Accomplished drivers became local legends and were admired for their daring. Many of them died in car crashes or were arrested playing cat-and-mouse with the law. The skilled driving they developed to elude revenue agents and transport moonshine to markets as far away as the coastal cities would later become a professional racing sport know as NASCAR.

The state and federal governments tried to stop illegal production of alcohol, in part to ensure that liquor was safe as well as taxed. Revenuers were assigned to go after the moonshiners, but as far as the government was concerned, bootleggers were the real problem. Once moonshine was sold, the government missed out on the tax revenue it collected on illegally distilled liquor.

This battle to collect taxes and the moonshiner's determination to avoid paying them was at the heart of the struggle between moonshiners and the law, and it dated back to the Whiskey Rebellion of 1794 when the Pennsylvania farmers rebelled against liquor taxation. Although the government won that battle, many of these farmers left Pennsylvania and came to the mountains of North Carolina to escape this perceived tyranny. And they did escape it, for the most part, making their liquor as they pleased without penalty for almost another century. When the railroad opened the door to forced taxation, a new phase of rebellion was unleashed and evasion was fueled by the automobile.

During Prohibition, this type of rebellion held popular sentiment. Robert's parents were not stigmatized by friends and neighbors for being in the illegal whiskey trade. Strangely enough, little Robert was born into a family of relative wealth. His father, Asbury, had a good job on the railroad, supplemented by the "family business" which was managed in his absence by his wife, Cora Belle, a skilled bootlegger in her own right and a woman of many talents. As a young girl she had been sent out to work at the Biltmore Estate for Edith Vanderbilt when Cornelia Vanderbilt was coming of age. She'd started as a scullery maid in the kitchens and rose in position to chef's assistant, learning to cook and manage a kitchen from some of the best culinary experts in the country. When she left there to marry Asbury, young Cornelia presented her with a string of pearls as a parting wedding gift.

Working on the estate had left its mark on her. She was ambitious for a better life but also knew the limitations imposed by her status. So she broke through them assisting her husband in a family enterprise that enabled them to live more prosperously than their peers and fostered a high opinion of herself and her children. With her skills as a manager and cook, she ran a boarding house that catered to travelers and temporary workers on the estate. Her home also served as an ideal distribution center with its hidden root cellars and built-in customer base. Many of her boarders were steady customers and she had a widespread circle of buyers who communicated their needs through message carriers and scheduled supply dates. Their eldest son, Rudolph, had been running liquor since he was twelve years old. Younger sisters Hazel and Jesse Mae were less involved, having been given the responsibility of taking care of baby Robert, making sure he was well-tended and spoiled.

Even as a toddler, Robert was taught to believe he was special. Everyone in the family turned their attention toward him and his every wish was granted. He was a pretty baby, strong and healthy and quick to learn. When he didn't get his own way, his fiery temper made its presence known. He was then appeased and applauded for having an Irish spirit and encouraged to vent his aggressions outdoors.

His father taught him to hunt, fish, and live off of the land when he was just a boy, taking him deep into the woods and challenging him beyond his years. Sometimes he would lie on his stomach beside his father behind a fallen log, their eyes and ears alert, watching and listening for the slightest movement or sound. And then, in an instant, his father's finger would press down on the trigger and his targeted game would be taken down. Robert would be filled with intense excitement, eager to have his turn.

Sometimes his older brother would join them and they would spend days and nights in the forest during the autumn deer hunting season. Like the hunters of old, his father would build a "closed camp," a half-faced cabin of logs, the front entirely open and the roof covered with hemlock boughs and tree bark, the inside lined with dried leaves and more hemlock and blankets. A fire would be built in front of the opening to warm them throughout the night.

His father taught them how deer could be tricked by using a method called "shining the eyes." He would affix a pan full of pine nuts, blazing from the fire, to a square wooden platform strapped to a stick. He'd then order one of them to take it and move quickly through the forest holding it up high. This could also be done on horseback if they were at lower elevations or on more level ground. The movement created a stream of light that could easily be followed by those watching with rifles prepared for action. If deer were sleeping in a nearby thicket, they would be awakened by the rustling sounds and mesmerized by the bright flickering glare moving through the dark trees. Instead of running, they would stand immobilized as perfect targets.

Robert learned many tricks from his father and even invented some of his own. With each passing year, he became more and more inclined to go off hunting by himself or take his own followers with him. He was accustomed to having people do what he wanted and assumed a leadership role with his friends. He was big for his age and naturally authoritarian.

When he reached the age of twelve, his fascination turned toward the river and the adventure it promised, particularly in the direction of the Biltmore Estate. The French Broad River bordered the estate and then cut through the middle of it as it came into confluence with Hominy Creek from the western side and the Swannanoa River, which flowed into it from the eastern side where the castle was located. Robert could walk to the French Broad River from his home and spent many hours fishing there. But he grew restless when he looked downriver and felt compelled to travel down its winding curve to the estate grounds where he was forbidden to go.

Determined to follow his impulses, he constructed a makeshift raft by nailing boards together and sealing them with tar. He then carved out a twelve foot pole to maneuver it and found an alcove under an overhang of vines and draping pines where he could hide it. There were several mishaps and repairs to the raft before he mastered the art of poling. He also learned the hard way to avoid using it after heavy rains when the river current was rushing high. After he familiarized himself with the three mile stretch of river that took him across the estate boundary line, he began to search for an advantageous spot to gain safe access to the western side of the Pisgah forest. He chose a place where the river was bordered on both sides by tall trees, rocky banks, and uneven ridges that kept him hidden from view. There, he banked his homemade craft and headed in the direction of the dense green forest that would swallow him into a shelter of protection.

He'd been warned over and over to stay away from the government-regulated forest. Trespassing and poaching were serious offenses and a team of game wardens monitored the area, headed by a wily forest ranger named Claude Austin. But Robert was too tempted and he'd heard too many stories listening to the boarders his mother served at dinnertime. All they ever talked about were the comings and goings at the Biltmore Estate—its village, dairy, and farms. They told of private hunting parties and the abundance of game and the special cooperation that existed between estate and forest management.

What really bothered him was the fact that the estate people had special privileges and organized hunts were going on all the time on the Biltmore Estate forestlands. They even used the forest rangers to set up stands and spook the game in the direction of the hunt. He thought it the height of hypocrisy, just like Prohibition; he'd made enough bootlegged deliveries to people who supported or enforced the liquor laws to know that there was a different law for the privileged than the poor. He learned that the only way to get one over on them was to have inside information. So, he made good use of what he overheard from the boarders to plan his excursions across the estate boundaries and into the forest. He also knew how to keep his own counsel and rarely confided in others. When he went on his solitary adventures downriver, no one was made aware of his plans.

Robert forged his own trail through an entangled thicket that grew along the riverbank and up toward the direction he had chosen. He marked his way with a hunter's skill. He didn't have to venture far to find hunting grounds that yielded him enough game to help his mother feed the family and boarders for a week. From then on, he made regular poaching trips during times when his father was away and his brother was on the road delivering moonshine. He created his own trailheads and was careful to camouflage them after entering and leaving, rotating his use of them so that no one trail revealed evidence of regular use.

He taught himself to build better rafts and then a small boat which he kept chained under an old split birch tree that had hidden space under its fallen limbs; he draped it with pine branches for added cover. Although he was cautious, he developed a passion for the risk involved in these undertakings and it became an obsession, fostering a multitude of minor feats of ingenuity. The estate forest had become his personal hunting grounds and it was a place that fed his need for excitement and growing desire for the adrenaline rush he felt when breaking the law.

Robert enjoyed contributing to the family by doing something other than bootlegging and expected praise for what he brought home. At age fifteen, he thought of himself as a man and wanted to prove himself in his own way. Although his mother was at first surprised, she hadn't questioned him when he came home with his kill. If she suspected he was poaching, it was best left unsaid. He'd learned early to dissuade her and others from rebuking him for anything he did. Besides, when it came to food, the old adage "Never look a gift horse in the mouth" applied, and the game he brought home was always appreciated.

Initially, he was content to poach only small game. It was easier to bag and carry out and get rid of quickly if necessary. But the idea of bringing out large game began to fuel his imagination. He started working on a boat that could carry a heavier load and adapted his hunting practices to this new self-challenge. He went on scouting expeditions to locate the territory of the big game he had in mind, the dangerous and reclusive black bear.

His quest for finding the black bear habitat led him to higher ground, up to the mountain ridges and cavernous areas, increasing his level of risk significantly. He explored sections where bear would most likely hibernate and tested how much time it took him to get in and out of the forest from these places and back upriver. He calculated the distance from where he was exploring to forest areas most frequented by game wardens. He kept himself updated on activities going on within the estate grounds and beyond and stayed alert to any changes that might hinder his planning. And then he waited for the autumn season to come, before the end of September when the leaves would begin to fall and the air would be clear and dry.

Robert couldn't take the chance of bringing in his father's Plott hounds to search for bear tracks. They were great bear hunting dogs but a luxury he could not afford in this situation. He'd been taught how to look for bear tracks in the wet sand and soil along the shorelines of mountain streams and how to seek out their food source in areas with a sufficient forage base, water supply, and good cover. He'd spent days trekking up and down steep ridges following waterways and drainages along the hollows and creeks and searching for nesting areas and caves along these narrow movement corridors. He studied the ground, looking for fresh scat, and scanned the trees, looking for claw marks on the tall oaks and mature poplars. He knew that lasting scars indicated a history of bear presence and anything fresh was cause for alert; they could climb trees easily and thrash through a stand of oaks tearing at branches with their strong claws and leaving behind a battered scene of wreckage. They were unpredictable and ferocious, the males weighing up to 300 pounds, with the ability to sprint up to 35 miles an hour.

He stalked his prey with a natural quiet stealth that gave him an extra edge in the forest. But the bear also had an edge, with its remarkable sense of smell and uncanny hearing ability. He could imagine a bear standing on his hind legs, sniffing the air for the scent of food and picking up his scent. So he was watchful, silent, and never let down his guard. His search paid off when he came across several unmistakable five-digit full-footed tracks that suggested their whereabouts. He made his way back along the lengthy trail he'd carefully marked, having established a starting point for his return. He knew it would be very dangerous to hunt the bear alone, but he didn't care; he was single-minded about what he wanted to do and had to prove to himself that it could be done. But another year would pass before he could pursue his quest.

Robert's plan was evolving at the same time conditions were changing in the forest and a higher level of security was being put in place by the government's Forestry Service. European expansion and settlement in western North Carolina had taken its toll on bear populations in the latter part of the 19th century when many forested areas were converted into agricultural croplands. Settlers had considered black bears such a threat to livestock that killing had been intensive and unregulated, nearly eradicating the bear population. Extensive logging that took place during the early part of the twentieth century had clear cut and destroyed vast areas of timber and obliterated the bear habitat. To make matters worse, in 1925, blight struck the chestnut trees. The American chestnuts had provided a consistent and abundant food supply for bears and other wildlife throughout the fall and winter months.

George Vanderbilt's conservation efforts, however, had

taken hold and recovery was evident, although virtually all of the mature chestnut trees had died as a result of the blight. The black bear survived the devastation and chestnut deprivation by slowly adapting within the improved conditions and moving to higher ground, clawing out dens in trees and caves up to 60 feet high and living on acorns, grasses, grasshoppers, ants, fruits, fish, and small mammals, all of which were thriving in this new habitat. Now the bears were thriving again, too, like the deer and wild turkey and fish in the teeming streams, because Pisgah's plants and wildlife were now in protected land.

Private government mountain land had a different meaning to Robert. He'd grown up listening to his father tell tales of legendary Appalachian bear hunters like Tom Wilson and his son, "Big Tom", who were renowned for killing hundreds of bears during their lifetimes in the late 1800s and early 1900s. He couldn't relate to the plight of the black bear. He'd been taught to hunt as a way of life and felt he had a right to hunt the forest lands without restriction, just like the frontiersmen who came before him.

Robert believed that no one man or government should hold ownership over that much wilderness, especially at a time when there was so much poverty. Not that he had ever been poor, but he knew many who were—many of his friends and neighbors, and now his own father had to work far away from home just to keep his job on the railroad. He was beginning to form immature stubborn and defiant conclusions about life and about himself, one of which was that he was just as good as any Vanderbilt, or any man for that matter, and more clever than most. He was on a path of self-delusion that would lead him into serious trouble.

About to turn sixteen, Robert had grown tall and strong, with thick wavy dark hair and piercing blue eyes. His slender long legs moved with graceful agility which enhanced his prowess as a hunter and as an athlete. His athleticism, however, was not directed into organized sports but instead into running from law enforcement, in one form or another. The game wardens were on to him, and highway revenuers were watching for him everywhere. He had gradually taken over his brother's local liquor routes and more and more of his father's responsibilities. He'd become less solitary as his self-confidence and reputation grew. He even managed to do well at school despite missing days at a time when he had more important things to do. At night, he drove along the mountain roads like a roaring wind and on weekends hunted where he pleased, often leading his friends into the forest to share in his bounty, daring them to enter into his adventures.

The days of hunting and fishing with his father were over and had been for years. But events that would change him from a young rebel into an identified outlaw were about to happen and he was not in the least prepared for it. He was on a collision course not only with the law, but also with life as he knew it.

During this time, Prohibition had ended and the Great Depression had taken hold of the country. These were desperate times. The railroad had cut its workforce and those who still had jobs had to travel greater distances to keep them. His father was often gone for months at a time, his older brother had left home, and his two sisters had married. Robert's wild streak found its outlet taking greater risks poaching the Biltmore forest and racing through the Buncombe County back roads. There were other options being presented to him in high school, but he paid little attention to them. He gave his future little thought because his needs had always been met within his home and surrounding environment.

The day of his mother's accident came as shock and a blow to his foundation of security. During Asbury's frequent absences, out of necessity Cora Belle had learned how to drive the family vehicle, a fairly new Packard. Driving along a Carolina back road, she swerved to avoid a car coming around a blind curve on her side of the road. The car hit a tree, preventing it from dropping into a deep ravine, which would have probably resulted in her death. Instead, she suffered severe injuries that left her permanently disabled and required her to use a cane and back brace for the rest of her life.

During her first month of recovery, Cora Belle was attended to by her daughters, Hazel and Jesse Mae. Asbury was granted time off from the railroad to come home and care for her. But it was apparent upon his return that his interest was focused elsewhere. He was ill-tempered and impatient, particularly with Robert. Asbury had always had periods of moodiness and Robert

had learned as a boy not to question him when it was not welcomed. This time, however, his father seemed different, strange.
He was not only preoccupied, he was coldly unsympathetic to
Cora Belle, and rarely made eye contact with Robert, who felt
confused and bewildered. He'd expected some acknowledgement from his father for the way he'd been taking care of his
mother. After all, he had been putting himself at risk keeping the
homestead well-stocked with game and had assumed the burden of responsibility for the care of the property in his father's
absence. But Asbury spoke not a word of gratitude nor did he
give Robert any signal of approval.

When Asbury left home abruptly without a word to anyone,
Robert could hardly believe it. For the first time in his life, he
felt rejected and entirely alone. He may have acted like a loner,
but he'd always felt his father's presence, even when he'd been
working far away from home. His father's authority, his rules,
and his way of doing things stayed behind after his departure;
how to care for his hounds, the correct way to hold an ax, the
best way to hone in on a target, the proper way to string a line,
everything remained but his presence. As strong as his mother
had been, she had always deferred to his father, and not one of
his children had ever treated him with disrespect. Robert had
grown taller than Asbury by inches, but had still looked up to
him, still needed his praise, his simple nod of approval. And now
he was gone with not even a word of farewell.

Left with too much responsibility, no explanation, and a
houseful of women who were tearful and distraught, Robert
felt angry and overwhelmed. And then the explanation came by
post, cruel and abbreviated. When his mother read the letter,
she cried out a scream of pain that sent shivers through his spine
and caused one of his sisters to fall into a dead faint. When Robert took the letter from his mother's trembling hands and read
it, he exploded with rage. Months of confusion were cleared up
in a few short barely legible sentences written in Asbury's hand
informing Cora Belle that he was living with another woman, in
another county, and would not be coming home ever again.

The sobbing of his mother and sisters for the next few days
drove him nearly mad. Robert's anger was visceral and he could
not communicate with anyone, much less give comfort. He went

hunting instead, just looking for something to kill, and would have killed his own father if the man had magically appeared before him. He was in an unknown wilderness of soul and spirit, filled with hatred and hurt so gut-wrenching that he could not eat or sleep or find his way out of it. His father had abandoned him as surely as he had his mother. It was a betrayal that he would never forgive and he swore to himself that he would forgive no other betrayal in his life that followed, no matter how slight.

His father's act of betrayal grew in his mind like an intangible monster that he could not kill and it was tearing him apart inside. But there was one monster that he could kill, and it was as black as the deed that had been done. Robert had been tracking the great elusive bear for the past several months, had sensed the might of the beast, and envisioned its unusually large size by the gigantic tracks it had left behind. Robert set his mind to go after it, and in doing so, redirected his pain into the hunt he was about to begin.

CHAPTER FIVE

> Whoever appeals to the law against his fellow man is either a fool or a coward
> Whoever cannot take care of himself without that law is both
> For a wounded man shall say to his assailant,
> "If I Live, I will kill you. If I Die, You are forgiven."
> Such is the Rule of honor.
> Broken the paradigm an example must be set.
> Invoke the Siren's song and sign the death warrant.
> This is what has been wrought for 30 pieces of silver.
> The tongues of men and angels bought by a beloved betrayer.
> I am the result, what's better left unspoken.
> Violence begins to mend what was broken . . .
> Omerta
>
> —*Lyrics by Lamb of God*, Omerta

The hunt began where it had left off before everything happened. It was later in the season and the bear would soon be hibernating in his cave for the winter. The leaves had fallen into a thick carpet beneath Robert's feet, slick and damp from a recent rainfall. The sun had risen steady and bright all morning, occasionally blinding him with streaking rays that cut through the shadowy pines. He shielded his eyes with his hand before looking upward toward the ragged rock cliffs he was about to climb. From there he would have a better view and the added advantage of height. The leaves had made tracking more difficult but he'd been near this area before and had found the unusually large tracks leading in the direction he was headed. He'd already found places in laurel thickets under fallen timbers where the sizable beast had bedded down for the night. Robert was in *his* territory now and the evidence was scarred into the trees and crushed into the sodden earth where he'd prowled and barreled his way to the high cavernous cliffs ahead.

His rifle was loaded and his Bowie knife sheathed to his belt. His anticipation grew as he sensed the bear's presence, not because of any sound or sign of movement but rather an innate sense of closeness to his prey. It was as if they knew of each other's existence and general whereabouts. He'd heard of such things from his father but this was his first experience of knowing it to be true. He reflected on his father's words and realized that his stories and lessons would always be with him, a constant reminder of what he had lost. How different it would be if he had lost him in death instead of dishonor. This thought caused his jaws to clench and his eyes to sting and his fist to close tightly around his gun.

The climb was strenuous and challenging but there were signs of previous climbs; the branches growing out from stonewall cracks and along cliff edges were snapped and broken and rocks were scattered along worn pathways that gradually weaved upward. There were sections of smooth faced rock that jutted up vertically, peaking into jagged precipices and crevices that opened to deep wells of darkness. Gaining a foothold an inch at a time in these places took longer than he had calculated and the sun moved over the sky with more progress than he was making. This did not bode well for a return to his makeshift camp before nightfall. He began taking chances, and at one point almost lost his footing on a rocky ledge that crumbled beneath his boot.

When he finally reached a platform of sizable proportion that gave him a solid base, he unstrapped the rifle from his chest and the sacking from his back and positioned himself on this lookout. From there he could see dark openings and indentations along uneven rock formations, indicating a series of caves above and beyond in the craggy surfaces. The massive boulder on which he stood was lodged against a vertical flat rock wall that leaned over the boulder like a partial shelter, casting a shadow that protected him from view. Enormous irregular-shaped rocks branched outward and upward at odd angles and elevations like missile projectiles being launched from behind the overhanging wall. It was a backdrop remnant of centuries-old volcanic eruptions, the jutting rocks divided by deep channels and narrow tunnels, passageways through which even a large animal could crawl from one side of the stony ridge to the other.

He walked over to the opposite side of the boulder from where he had ascended and looked over the edge. There was a steep drop-off to a shallow wooded valley bathed in golden sunlight that streamed down from the western sky. To the left of him he could see a crevice opening and a path-worn ledge leading down to the valley. It explained why he'd lost the bear's tracks right before he made it to the lookout and how the bear had reached his final destination. The valley seemed a perfect haven for the bear to be milling around and he began his watch by scanning the lower area for signs of movement.

It was getting late. The setting sun began to cut horizontally through the shadow of the overhang, warming the surface of the smooth rock platform and his back as he crouched there looking down. The warmth would soon be gone and everything would grow cold and perilous. He'd stay a short time longer, then begin his descent. Only a few more minutes passed before he heard the sound. It was only a slight grunt, but it was unmistakable. It seemed to come from somewhere below him, but he knew that sound traveled like echoes in the higher elevations and he wasn't sure where to look first.

In heightened expectation, he focused his attention down to a cluster of rhododendrons near an opening in a stand of pines. He thought he'd seen movement, but nothing stirred. He leaned forward over the edge, trying to see through the mountain laurel that grew outward from an inversion underneath the ledge, but saw nothing. The stillness that followed was like a stopped heartbeat, breath held, life depending on the next beat. When he heard it again, there was no sigh of relief or time to breathe again because the sound was closer and behind him instead of down where he'd been looking. The bear's scent filled his nostrils. He turned around just in time to see the black inside of the bear's ear as it flicked and glistened in the sun. His great head emerged from below the other side of the boulder. Through the afternoon glare he could see the monstrous black creature climb onto the platform only a few yards away from him. His ears were pinned down to his skull and his eyes were intensely focused on his intended victim. Then he let out a low, almost guttural sound while popping his teeth together like a percussionist would a set of drumsticks before starting a high energy performance.

He couldn't believe it! The bear must have been following him all along, climbing steadily behind him, returning to the place where he knew his pursuer would be trapped. It was impossible, such planning, such entrapment, and yet here he was with nothing between them but the barrel of his rifle and a knife on his belt. He had no room to move, nowhere to go except a fall backward to his death or a move forward into the black mass of destruction.

The bear let out an earsplitting roar that expelled a flood of hot breath that reached him before the bear charged with teeth bared, hungry for blood. In a fast direct motion, Robert lunged forward with the rifle barrel, thrusting it into the bear's growling throat. The gun fired and blood spurted back out from the howling abyss covering him with a film of red. But the bear didn't stop, bowling him over and grabbing and pulling him in close with his powerful forearms, intending to bite repeatedly until death overtook one of them. Robert tried to reach for the knife but was impeded by thrashing claws and muscle reflexes that denied the deadly wound. When his hand found the knife and he managed to pull it from the sheath, it took all of his strength to jab it into the side of his heaving dying adversary, both of them bloody and torn. The knife went in again and again until the horror was over and the bear was dead.

Robert lay there, barely able to move, blood soaked but breathing again, grateful to be alive. His injuries were mainly torn flesh on his arms, chest and throat, and a head wound that felt swollen and raw. He suffered no broken bones, which probably saved his life because he wouldn't have been able to manage his way back down the steep incline. He cut up his shirt with his bloody knife and stopped the bleeding where he could. And then in an act of sheer willpower and dexterity, he skinned the bear where it fell and loaded the hide and what remained of the head into the sacking he had brought with him. There would be no return for the meat; this had not been a hunt for food. It had been a hunt for his manhood and it wasn't over yet. He strapped the heavy sack onto his naked back and began his descent under a darkening sky. He'd be lucky to make it back to his camp alive.

He did make it back, back from the forest and back from the depths of despair. After a night of painful encampment tending his wounds to stave off infection, and a dawn trip back to the boat that tested every ounce of his endurance, he maneuvered up the river as if in a dream. It was a dream where he was the hero, a frontiersman from days of old, a superior man who recognized no king other than himself, who would make his own way in life, and do it *his way*. The boat floated high above the river and he could see the vast land around him as it once was, free to anyone who could meet its challenge. Even the Cherokees had never understood the concept of land ownership, never thinking they could own the wilderness, thinking it a gift lent to them by their gods. And his God had created him, not to be inferior to people with money and power, people who tried to deny him his right to the land and the bounty he deserved. And in the dream, which might have been a hallucination, he saw an eagle soar alongside him and felt at one with the majestic bird.

When he approached the homestead with his wounded body and heavy burden, he was ready to face the pain and sorrow awaiting him there. However, the screams he would hear this time would be for the state of his condition and the mending he would need—women's work, he thought, to vanquish the tears of his sisters and shock his mother into beginning her fight back to life without a husband who wasn't worth weeping over.

And they did tend to him, and treated him as they always had, the center of their attention. His recovery was quick, leaving a few physical scars. But it was the psychological change in him that was more apparent. He no longer had to prove himself to anyone and the scars from his battle were worn like a badge of honor. The cocky self-assurance he had always possessed was infused with a new dimension of pride. He had a winning personality when he wanted to turn it on, but there was a hint of menace right below the surface that would appear when he wanted to intimidate someone, adding to his air of authority.

He'd become ambitious, and more interested in his final year of high school. His friends there were followers rather than buddies and most of them were sons of men of influence. They'd admired him before because he'd had access to the best booze and had given them an outlet for the excitement they craved. He'd always seemed much older to them, but now he was changed in ways they couldn't understand. His friends outside of school were mostly dropouts, uneducated, from poorer mountain families, but clever in ways that his friends at school could not imagine. They drove the back roads and roamed the backwoods and piloted the backwaters with him as knowledgeably as any metropolitan gang knew their inner-city territories. And they helped him to keep his school buddies supplied with liquor and outdoor adventure.

Robert was building a network to serve his future interests, but something bigger was brewing for all of them, high risk adventures they never could have dreamed of were coming their way. They were all around age 17 and the year was 1941.

CHAPTER SIX

For the strength of the Wolf is the Pack and
the strength of the Pack is the Wolf.
—Rudyard Kipling

On the morning of December 7th, 1941, the Japanese Imperial Navy represented by 353 Japanese fighters, bombers and torpedo planes, launched from six aircraft carriers in two waves a surprise military strike on the naval base at Pearl Harbor, Hawaii. As a result 2,402 Americans were killed and 1, 282 were wounded. The attack came as a profound shock to the American people and led directly to the American entry into World War II in both the Pacific and European theaters. The following day, December 8, the United States declared war on Japan. The lack of a formal warning by the Japanese, particularly while negotiations were ongoing, led President Franklin Delano Roosevelt to proclaim December 7th, 1941 "a date that will live in infamy."

For young men like Robert and his friends, whether rich or poor, this was a call to arms. Some enlisted immediately, others finished school and were promptly drafted. Those who were denied for physical or mental reasons felt ashamed and frustrated. It was that kind of war.

Robert knew that military draft was imminent after he received his diploma. It couldn't have come at a better time because the head forest ranger, Claude Austin, who had been chasing him for the past two years, had finally caught him as a result of a fluke incident. He'd been hunting alone for some quick small game too near the logging roads he usually avoided. But he'd heard that a hunting party was going out from the estate that day and he wanted to take advantage of the game being flushed. He knew how to keep his distance from the party and profit from the hunt, but he hadn't realized that Claude Austin had caught on to his habit of benefiting from their efforts. So when he heard the squeaky springs of Austin's old Buick, a sound he recognized from previous close encounters with the ranger, he hunkered down behind a cluster of laurel and waited for the car to move on up the road.

When the Buick stopped and the engine was turned off, Robert's pulse quickened and he figured he'd better start running. Claude was behind him in a minute and had already radioed in for assistance. The rangers nearby responded, closing in on him like a gauntlet, but he managed to avoid capture by weaving around them. Another small group of rangers who were waiting ahead converged upon him and he was caught. Unfortunately for Austin, he hadn't had the chance to shoot any game and could only be charged with trespassing. Nevertheless, Austin had him taken into custody and held under suspicion of poaching, although in this instance it couldn't be proven. Robert was placed in the county lock-up to await a morning hearing that would determine his fine.

For the second time in his life, Robert felt tricked and trapped. He also felt humiliated and intensely angry, but not the least bit afraid. Before the day was out, he'd contacted a friend whose father had some pull with the magistrate and was released with a warning and no fine. This pat on the wrist infuriated Austin, who immediately took steps to ensure that Robert was listed as a suspected felon on the State Registry of Offenders, thereby labeling him an *outlaw* (a legal term that was still on the books in western North Carolina), as far as the government was concerned. Robert sensed it was time to leave — his current habitat was getting too hot, even for him; so he enlisted in the Navy.

He would soon be in a place much hotter. It was the early years of World War II and he was right in the midst of it. If he had thought of himself as special before he entered the military, it was proven to him by the testing he received at the Naval Academy. He scored so high that he was sent to be trained as a cryptographer. He was then assigned to serve under Admiral Nimitz, who took a liking to him and recommended him for the Office of Strategic Services (OSS). The OSS was an agency of the Joint Chiefs of Staff, charged with collecting and analyzing strategic information and secret intelligence required for military operations, and with planning and executing programs of physical sabotage and morale subversion against the enemy to support military operations.

The OSS was dynamic and constantly changing in scope of activity, continually adapting to the needs of the war and to peculiar conditions in the various theaters of operations. Robert was in his element in any situation requiring on the spot ingenuity, innovation, and invention and it wasn't long before he had set up his own communications signals network. Amazed at his abilities, his commanding officer once questioned him,

"Where do you mountain boys get your know-how?"

He'd just laughed in response, but thought to himself, *Where indeed?*

By using skills and talents previously applied within the intricate web of secret mountain communication supporting illegal activities, Robert transposed and advanced them into strategic actions that served his country well, sending and receiving messages that helped in the killing of General Yamamoto. He was commended for his performance and when released from combat operations, was sent to college at North Carolina State and then to the University of North Carolina at Chapel Hill, where he received a military-financed education. Ironically, he graduated with a degree in *Wildlife Management*.

When Robert returned to Buncombe County, he was in the process of finalizing his education, living away on campus most of the time. He came home a decorated World War II veteran with an imposing 6 foot, 3 inch muscular frame, walked with a swagger and had a ready smile. His character had changed only in that every aspect of it was enhanced; the good and the bad, the bad masked in sly humor and wicked charm. Asheville had become a bustling city and he cruised around town on warm summer evenings, scouting the territory and hooking up with old friends.

This would become a ritual for young men in the approaching era of the 1950s, but the war decade hadn't ended yet and the sacrifices endured and losses sustained were still fresh in the minds of the people. The southern mountain regions had traditionally given more than their fair share of sons to war efforts, dating back to Revolutionary and Civil War times when their sharp-shooting abilities were demanded. World War II was no exception.

Those who did return were greeted as heroes and Robert took full advantage of his newfound popularity. Asheville was his new hunting grounds now, and he maneuvered through town like he had through the forest, with a hunter's keen eye and a definite purpose. He didn't frequent liquor houses, night clubs, or other local dens of iniquity. He'd seen enough of that before and during the war and he'd had his fill. He wasn't attracted to the wild side of life when it came to women; he thought too much of himself and they presented no challenge, an essential stimulus to his mind and libido. He was on a quest for a mountain princess and he found her sitting on a stool in a soda fountain drug store on the main street of West Asheville. She was almost sixteen and fresh as the mountain air, sweet and pretty, churchgoing and pure, and she looked at him with adoration in her eyes.

Her name was Nancy Anne Stanton (she preferred Anne) and she lived on the other side of the mountain from Robert's homestead. Her father was a respected attorney with ties to the Asheville legal system and city hall, her mother, a gracious homemaker who was beloved by her husband. This was a problem for Robert, considering his background. Anne's parents were on a higher social level and her father had connections to people he'd had run-ins with, both from his bootlegging days and later incidents. Beyond that, Robert's father had disgraced the family, and his mother was working on the Biltmore Estate again, cooking for the government workers. He was seven years older than Anne and knew that he would not be considered suitable by her parents. This only made him want her more. And since he recognized no person as being in a class above him, he ignored the obstacles that stood between them and made her believe she had met her prince charming.

Anne started meeting with Robert in secret, knowing that her father would never approve. Her love for him grew during the passionate brief encounters they shared. While she finished high school and he continued his university education, Robert engaged in other activities during semester breaks. He hadn't forgotten that Ranger Claude Austin had gotten the best of him and despite all his worldly adventures and experiences, he wasn't about to let that go. He was back into poaching again, and this time with a long-term plan.

His mother, Cora Belle, remained partially disabled but had managed to obtain a position on the estate due to her culinary reputation. This was perfect for Robert because she fed him information and he learned about the mountain-top hunting lodge that had been built near the Pisgah School of Forestry. Because of the co-operation between estate and forest management, Cora Belle often worked at the lodge during hunting season. On breaks from school, Robert found out from her what was going on up there and formed his own hunting parties when the lodge was full and the rangers were busy keeping track of the hunters who held special permits.

Robert had learned a lot working with OSS during the war, particularly about black market operations and counter-espionage. He wasn't about to let that knowledge go to waste. He started with a small band of trusted friends from the old days and added to them from his new Asheville acquaintances. Some of his Chapel Hill university friends were studying law and had summer jobs working in Asheville for attorneys or politicians who were part of the old boy network that ran things in the county. Robert supplied them with moonshine whiskey and illegal hunting experiences and they supplied him with information and new contacts.

Asheville was still a constrained society with a young adult population trying to break through the restraints. Power was wielded by an older established order that maintained without flexibility their rigid outdated rules. Class distinctions, discriminations, corporal punishments, and even dress codes were dictated as unchangeable laws. But a post war generation that had seen and experienced life beyond these boundaries—those who had rebelled early, like Robert, or rebelled later, like many of his followers—were biting at the bit, eager to kick the foundation from underneath those in control. Rock and roll was on the horizon, but for the time being, rebellion was done in the dark and in out-of-the-way places, in mouth-to-ear communications, and by running away to escape.

For Robert and Anne, the decision was made after two incidents that brought their relationship into the light of day. The first happened as a result of information that alerted Ranger Claude Austin to Robert's activities. He'd set a trap for Robert but managed to catch only one member of his hunting group, who later informed on Robert after being questioned for hours. The following day, Robert was served with a warrant for his arrest. When the news made the papers, Anne tried to contact him without success and in a panic of concern, asked her father to help Robert, and admitted to their relationship. Her father responded with fury and threatened to shoot Robert on sight. When Robert learned what had happened, he convinced Anne to run away with him and defy everyone by getting married. They left for South Carolina the next day, bought a permit for one dollar, and were married in the Pickens County Courthouse.

By the time Anne's parents found out about the marriage, Robert and Anne were in California. In a letter to them, Anne pleaded for understanding and declared her undying love for Robert. Her parents were devastated and convinced that their daughter had entered into a disastrous marriage. They were also wise and realized they would lose her if the marriage was not accepted. Her father wrote a letter back addressed to both of them, encouraging Robert to complete his education in California, and promised to welcome him back when they returned to North Carolina.

During their absence, Robert's legal issues were still pending and he'd been officially declared an "outlaw" by the executors of the Biltmore Estate. Cora Belle resigned from her job there and retired to the French Broad homestead, living on proceeds left over from the family business that she'd squirreled away in the root cellar for her later years. She had never fully recovered from her injuries or her own personal heartbreak. Robert, however, continued to be her pride and joy, despite his infamous status, and in her mountain circle of friends and relations he remained a legend, so she had no need to lower her head in shame.

Several years passed before Robert and Anne returned. By then, many things had been forgiven and forgotten. Ranger Claude Austin had retired and so had Anne's father. Anne had also changed. She'd matured into a beautiful woman but there was something missing from her spirit; the love-light that had once twinkled in her eyes like starlight was replaced by a hint of anxiety. Her sweet innocence was gone forever, replaced with a steady womanly resolve and practiced submissiveness. Robert, having earned a Masters Degree in biological engineering, had only grown in confidence.

Robert and Anne settled into the family homestead with his mother who, although infirm, was completely in charge of her domain. Robert had modeled his authoritarian manner after her. After several interviews, highlighting his impressive war record, he was hired by the U.S. Department of Agriculture as a biologist and was trained to be a seed inspector for the State of North Carolina. He pursued the departmental position to prevent being confined to a lab or an office. As regional inspector, he had freedom and flexibility, traveling throughout the state inspecting the seed products of mill merchants and farmers. He used some of this time to develop sideline businesses that gave him additional income. During the next several years he would start an airboat service piloting people up and down the French Broad River to view the Biltmore Estate, from a distance. His knack for boat building and love of the river had never left him and he parlayed them into a weekend business that coincided with his week-night hunting raids onto the estate grounds. Robert had worked out a deal in absentia related to the outstanding warrant against him and proceeded to use his connections to keep that problem in abeyance.

Cora Belle ran the household, enabling Anne to accept a secretarial job at the newly refurbished Buncombe County Courthouse in Asheville. Despite his retirement, her father was still held in high regard there, which helped her to obtain the position. Robert did not object to his wife working because it served his purposes and the added income helped to support his business ventures. Anne moved up rapidly through city hall secretarial ranks and her efficiency was noted by the newly elected District Attorney, Bob Swain. Swain had her transferred from the secretary pool into his office and elevated her to the status of assistant. This could not have been better for Robert. He learned through Anne that Swain was an avid hunter and it wasn't long before he and Robert were introduced and began sharing this common interest.

Robert was from mountain stock, born and bred, and carried on the tradition of multiple talents and trades. With Anne working and Cora Belle in charge of the household and a job in which he couldn't be pinned down as long as he completed his duties, he had time to develop his ideas independently. The Department of Agriculture provided him with many perks, travel expenses, automobile, work clothing, and other essentials that saved him money and cut his own expenses. Robert hated spending money when he could barter or beat someone out of a few dollars in a deal. His travels also helped him to expand his illegal trade customer base just as Cora Belle had done years before with bootlegging customers and the boarding house.

There was always the legitimate business on the surface that fronted for the illegitimate one that brought in untaxed income. Robert equated having to pay taxes with highway robbery and was determined to make back tax money one way or another. He harbored resentment for any person, organization, state or federal government entity that got the best of him financially. He'd been glad to serve his country during the war, but thought enough was enough when it came out of his wallet.

Besides, he now had his eye on a nearby tract of land with a large frame house on it that was about to be available for sale. He was becoming an astute land speculator, picking up tips about properties that were in tax arrears or foreclosure, tax sales loopholes, and other opportunities for picking up acreage cheap. He also decided that it was time to own a residence separate from his mother. Anne had been working for the D.A. for several years now and he told her she deserved something to show for her efforts.

The move into their home gave Anne a new spark to her personality but it also gave her a heavy load of responsibility. She was the woman of the house now instead of her mother-in-law.

Although she initially tried, she found housework overwhelming and Robert continually compared her unfavorably to his mother. Her cooking was never good enough to please him, although it improved significantly over the years. Robert didn't help because he saved everything and stored many of the acquisitions he would pick up here and there in the house like a packrat. He refused to spend money on anything but the bare essentials. He put his money into a multitude of ventures, one of them buying cars at auction and fixing them up for resale. He did the same with boats, farm equipment, or anything else he could turn over for ready cash. But the cash was never spent to lavish anything on Anne, and he resented anything that she spent on herself.

When Robert brought home friends to visit, Anne cooked for them and made them feel welcome. She listened to their conversations and sometimes gave input with tidbits of information from the courthouse. This was one area that Robert could not control and she knew he enjoyed letting his friends see the access he had through her. But he never let her feel good about it for very long. He liked to demonstrate to others that he was the man of the house and would often criticize her in front of them if she got too much attention. He had also engaged her boss, Bob Swain, in his unscrupulous activities after taking him on a few hunting trips.

Swain was a complex man who aspired to greatness but had the same temptations as others who fell under Robert's influence. Robert used this alliance as another avenue of control over Anne because he knew that she loved her job; it was her only escape from the home. Robert's relationship with her boss meant that every aspect of her life was under scrutiny. If Anne disagreed with him in any way, he put her "back in her place" by deriding her and chipping away at her confidence. Robert could not tolerate dissension. Sometimes he worried that she was getting ideas about equality at home and in the workplace from some of the hype that was going on in the media by women's rights groups.

His worries were relieved when she gave him the news that she was pregnant. He was elated that his purchase of the home had paid off in a way he hadn't planned and began to hope for a son. But it was not in his best interest for Anne to retire from the D.A.'s office, so she took a temporary maternity leave instead and then nestled into her home for the remainder of the pregnancy. Several months later she gave birth to an 8 pound 9 ounce baby boy. They named him Robert Jr. and would call him Bobby.

Robert now had a son.

CHAPTER SEVEN

What was for me a matter of course, that senseless asking for
water, and then the extraordinary terror of being carried outside were
two things that I, my nature being what it was, could never properly con-
nect with each other. Even years afterwards, I suffered from the torment-
ing fancy that the huge man, my father, the ultimate authority, would
come almost for no reason at all and take me out of my bed in the night
and carry me out onto the pavalatche, and that consequently I meant
absolutely nothing as far as he was concerned.
— Franz Kafka, "Letter to His Father"

"Bobby. Bobby! Get your butt over here, and hurry, boy. Don't just stand there. Grab his legs. Grab them! Help me drag him over to the ridge to that bank over there. I said move it, son!"

Bobby felt the fear and revulsion rise as he tried to compre-hend what was happening. He grabbed onto CB's heavy boots, but they were too big for his small hands to grip. He clutched onto the pant legs above the boot tops, his fingers straining to hold fast without dropping a leg as his father lifted and pulled CB's upper body across the open field. He thought he felt a slight jerking movement, but then it stopped.

Thoughts raced through his mind like a blurring wind that swept questions along in a rapid stream of consciousness. What had Daddy done? What was he, what were they, going to do? CB was his friend, their friend. Why did Daddy kill him? Was he really dead? Maybe he wasn't, maybe he was just foolin'. Maybe this was all a dream. Oh God, don't let me drop his legs. Oh Jesus, one of them is jerking again.

And while part of his mind was moving so fast he couldn't slow it down, another part was at a standstill in a space that had the answers, that knew; knew why it had happened and had known for some time that it would, ever since that day in the car.

"Pay attention, boy. Quit draggin' your feet. Help me get him over here. Don't be feelin' bad about this traitor. He got just what he deserved. Toughen up, boy."

The minutes went by like hours. He'd been left there on the bank of the ridge that was near the logging road where his father had driven away and would soon return. Left to guard the body while his father went to get help and report the accident; the accident that was no accident. He knew that help would be too late, that CB was already dead, and he had helped—maybe after the evil deed was done—but he had helped. He couldn't look at the man, the friend of his father's, his friend, who had been so kind to him, like no other man he'd known, except maybe his grandpa. But Grandpa Stanton was old and never came to their home to visit, and he wouldn't understand at all. He and Grandma were separate from all this, separate and unknowing about such things. Tears welled up in Bobby's eyes as he thought of his grandparents and what they would think of him if they knew what he'd done. He looked away from the body toward the forest in the distance where they'd been heading when it happened.

Suddenly he was startled to attention by a sound. Bobby couldn't move and sat frozen in terror. Oh my God, he thought, he isn't dead. The swelling went down from the man's esophagus and a gasp of air came out of him like a whoosh.

Oh God, he's still alive! A sudden realization came over Bobby. He knew what needed to be done, remembered what CB had once told him. He needed emergency medication, a doctor. Where was CB's emergency kit, the one with the medication that would save him? Bobby looked at the man's belt, where the kit had always been attached. It wasn't there. CB needed a tourniquet, but Bobby didn't know how to make one with what he had. He remembered some of the things he should do, but couldn't act.

The horrible sound propelled him to his feet. He stared down at CB, his eyes wide and terrified. Is he really alive? What if he is still alive? What will he do? Should I pick up a rock and hit him in the head, finish him like a lame animal? What should I do? What? What? He wanted to scream. Tears stung his cheeks and all he could do was stare. He stared until the silence lasted and no more sounds were emitted. He stared until he could finally move his eyes back to the forest where he wanted to run, to run into it and never come out again. He sat back down instead and continued to gaze hypnotically toward the trees, aching for their comfort, and the escape from CB's silent corpse.

The morning fog was lifting and the sun was breaking through it producing a steamy effect on the meadow grass and a smoky profusion of mist rising from the forest to the high mountains. The mist moved like a ghostly apparition and he imagined the life of CB rising with it, being taken up and enveloped into the mass of bluish clouds. He wondered if CB could see him, sitting there guarding his dead body. He'd never been so scared in his life and shut his eyes, trying not to see CB's spirit form in the movement, trying not to panic and run as fast as he could into the forest, into the mist, even knowing that CB might still be there hovering, waiting for him.

Another fear, more real, more threatening, stronger than his impulse to run, had a history that kept him from leaving the body. If his father returned and found him gone, there would be a punishment too awful to think about. It was better to stay put and think about CB floating in the forest or the mountain sky. It was better to remain in the living nightmare, intolerable as it seemed, and try to think about CB when he was alive.

There was one day that stood out in his memory and it came back to him clear and present because of its significance.

It was September, a bright cool autumn day with crisp leaves beginning to fall from the trees and colors changing all around him. Even at his young age, he thought the mountains in autumn had to be the most beautiful place on earth. Maybe it was because he spent so much of his time outdoors observing all that nature had to offer with his acute attention to detail and the watchful curiosity that had been his gift at birth. He'd been such an alert baby, sturdy and inquisitive, eager to crawl, walk, and then run outside into the fresh mountain air.

He'd been outside most of the day, playing near the house, when CB came driving down the long driveway in his El Camino. CB, his father, Julius, and his mother's boss, Bob Swain, had left early that morning to go dove hunting. His father had taken them to the un-opened portion of the Pisgah National Forest. The grass seeds that were sown that time of the year attracted doves by the hundreds. And, as always, the men had shot way over the legal limit. CB had left them early, due to a dinner date he had planned. Bobby often overheard his parents talk about CB being a ladies' man, always having two or three girls on the dangle.

Whenever CB had to leave early, Robert, the ring-leader of the group, sent him back to the house with the accumulated illegal kill so they could continue shooting. Bobby felt ecstatic to have the chance to help CB unload the trunk and to be alone with him for the short time he would be there.

CB got out of the car and called to him in his big boisterous voice, "Hey there, Little Bob. Come over here, boy, and give me a hug."

CB was a big man, warm and gregarious, and always dressed like a hunter out of a magazine, outfitted with the best Cabela hunting clothes and gear money could buy. He was a sight to behold as far as Bobby was concerned, no matter what he'd heard his father say about CB's dandified ways. Bobby didn't care because he idolized him, mainly because CB took the time to give him the positive attention he craved and it made him feel special. CB would look right at him and talk to him like he was important, even if he was just a kid.

When the sacks of birds were almost unloaded and hung in the barn, his mother called to them from the house. She'd been cooking deer meat and invited CB inside to eat. Recalling it, Bobby realized how odd it was that CB would eat a plate of deer meat before going on a dinner date. He hadn't thought of it at the time because he'd been so excited about CB visiting with them for a while. And he could tell that his mother was excited, too.

CB regaled them with stories of his adventures and bragged on his mother's cooking so much that her cheeks turned red as cherries. The time went by too quickly, and his stories were so fascinating, told in such a way that it left them yearning for more. It was like there was never enough time and everything was condensed into an hour or so—life, laughter and enjoyment—a rare event in that house, except when CB was there. It was as if CB knew he and his mother craved everything that he did. And then, when CB had to leave, there would be bear hugs for the both of them. He remembered his mother saying wistfully as CB walked away to his car, "He puts me in mind of Ernest Hemingway."

"Who's that, Momma?"

"Just another man who tells stories, Bobby. But his are better than most."

And then he'd be gone and they would both begin waiting for his next visit, without mentioning a word about it to anyone. It was a silent bond between them. Now it was making him sick thinking about it, that same sick feeling that he'd felt every time his father had said things about CB, things that he'd taken as a warning, ever since that day in the car.

He tried to recall: Was it later that fall, or was it early winter? No, it was a Sunday morning, the day before deer season opened, which by tradition was the third Monday in November, so it must have been November. He'd been with his Dad and CB, sitting in the back seat of the Plymouth, riding along Interstate 40 in an area that was lightly traveled during that time. He was supposed to be helping them to spot deer, with the objective being to shoot the deer from the car window. If one was hit, later that night, he would be sent with his older cousin, Hobart, his Dad's flunky, to retrieve it.

Instead of watching for deer, he was paying more attention to the conversation going on in the front seat between his Dad and CB and thinking how great it was to be doing something with them and how other kids, he'd bet, didn't get to do things like this with their Dads. But he did, and it almost made up for the other things his Dad made him do that he hated.

He remembered CB asking his Dad questions about the Davidson River trout stream that had been poisoned, but he'd thought nothing of it while listening to them discuss it. They continued riding for two or three more hours, not seeing any bucks to shoot. He had spotted a few does, but his Dad wouldn't shoot them because they fell into an illegal category. It would have been different if they'd been hunting in the depths of the forest. But on the interstate, in an area where deer were known to cross the highway, his father reasoned that they couldn't be arrested for breaking the law for shooting a buck, except for trespassing when they went to retrieve it, and since he wouldn't be the one doing that, he really couldn't be accused of breaking the law at all. This was just one of the skewed rationalizations he practiced to outwit law enforcement. It was like a game with him.

Heading back to Asheville, they dropped CB off where his car was parked in the Biltmore Village at a place called The Hot Shot Café, a popular local gathering spot in that part of town, Biltmore being a suburb of Asheville. When CB got out of the car, he'd moved from the back seat up to the front. His Dad didn't start the car but sat there watching CB walk towards his El Camino with a look on his face that filled him with dread. When his Dad finally spoke, he was still staring ahead, not seeming to notice that he was sitting there next to him.

"He's nothing but a lousy Judas. He's trying to find out if we poisoned the Davidson River."

"Find out for who, Daddy?" he'd timidly replied.

"Keep quiet, son, I wasn't talking to you."

So, he'd kept quiet, but felt all queasy inside, a sick awful feeling that CB was in trouble. The feeling came and went over the next several months but was more powerful each time he had it, like a surging river. It came whenever he'd see that look in his father's eyes, all mean and squinty, whenever CB turned his back. To CB's face, he'd act friendly, like everything was okay, and they continued to go hunting together, and with others, just as they had before. And when the feeling went away, it never went away completely. He'd think of it at bedtime and sometimes wake in the middle of the night from a bad dream, a dream of CB lying cold and dead on the ground. He could tell that his Dad no longer trusted CB and he knew what that meant. He'd seen what happened to others who got on his Dad's bad side. Like the night he'd gone deer hunting with his Dad and they were shooting near a neighbor's farm. When the neighbor heard the shooting, he called in a complaint and the Sheriff's deputy came out and did a half-hearted search for them in the dark but couldn't find them. After the deputy left, his Dad had said, "Come on, Bobby. We'll show him not to call the law on us."

They'd snuck onto his property and set his haystack on fire and then sat and watched as the man came running out in the middle of the night, screaming and carrying on and trying to put out the fire. At the time, he'd thought it funny and felt kind of proud that he and his Dad had done this chicanery together. But it didn't seem so funny anymore. It had only been a small fire, a minor payback. When CB mentioned what happened at the Davidson River and he'd seen his father's reaction, he'd instinctively known that CB had signed his own death warrant.

Bobby vividly remembered that morning on the Davidson River. It was the event that started everything. He recalled:

They'd gone on an overnight fishing trip. He remembered it as clear as day because it was the first time he'd been out all night camping with his Dad. He'd been much younger then, maybe five or six years old. Daddy had brought along Darrel, the son of his good friend Julius, and his cousin Hobart was supposed to meet up with them the next morning. Darrel was much older than he was, almost in his twenties.

They arrived at the gateway entrance to Pisgah Forest in the late afternoon and headed up the mountain road driving past the campground area. Daddy always knew the best places to hunt and fish and he didn't like other folks being around, except for those he invited along. They were going to camp farther up near the fish hatchery. The Davidson River was in Transylvania County, on the other side of the Pisgah Mountain from Buncombe County. The Davidson River ran down the mountain there, winding its way through the forest and the lower campground and beyond the gateway over through the town of Brevard.

According to Daddy, the middle part of the Davidson River that flowed between Avery Creek and the fish hatchery had a reputation for being one of the top fly fishing rivers on the east coast because of the amount of fairly large trophy winning trout, mainly brown trout. And the reason there were so many was because they were smart and cunning as a fox and that's why they'd survived all the fishing that went on there. He talked about the fish like he admired them.

He said they had to be careful coming into the forest on the gateway side because of the campers and tourists. The campground at the base of the mountain was just a little ways past the entrance and there was another one at the top of the mountain off the Blue Ridge Parkway by the old hunting lodge. The road they were on wound its way up to the parkway and the river ran alongside of it part of the way and at varying distances. The Davidson River was under the management of the U.S. Forest Service in cooperation with the North Carolina Wildlife Resources Commission and there were lots of rules and regulations. Daddy called it a State and Federal Government double whammy. There were green and white diamond-shaped signs posted by the campgrounds stating local fishing regulations. Daddy had stopped to read them on the way in. When he'd gotten back in the Plymouth, he'd acted purely disgusted.

There was a cut-off road that was barely noticeable and they almost missed it. The rough gravel road led to a secluded spot between the lower and middle Davidson River, not far from the hatchery. The forest was dark and dense along that section of the river until it opened up to a sunny clearing where the river widened and the water rippled slow and smooth over pebbles and stones and big sloping rocks. It was a perfect spot to set up camp for the night.

That night he'd been so excited he could hardly sleep. He listened to the night sounds and Daddy's quiet almost silent breathing and Darrel's occasional loud snoring for what seemed like hours. When he finally fell to sleep, it was a deep and dreamy slumber and he dreamt that he caught the biggest fish in the river and when he held it up for everyone to admire, he could see the proud look on his father's face. It was the best dream he'd ever had.

He awakened to the sound of Hobart's shout of arrival. The van pulled in slowly and Hobart parked it off to the side of their campsite. Hobart was supposed to be working. He worked for a pest control company in Asheville. The truck had a big black bug with wings and antennae painted on the side. After getting out of the van, Hobart opened the side door of it and showed them all the chemicals inside, and also the hidden compart-ments. They always had hiding places in their vehicles, some-times in the wheel wells and sometimes in places built into the paneling and under the flooring. They used the compartments for hauling liquor and hiding silencers, and that day, it would be used to hide the extra fish they caught so they could bring home a good catch. Daddy's idea of a good catch was bigger than what most people caught, and beyond the legal limit, and he and Hobart had a plan this time for netting a big haul.

Daddy had been reading about a tribe in South America who used some plant extract to pour into the river, just ahead of where the fish were upstream. After the fish swam through it, becoming momentarily paralyzed, the tribe would catch the season's supply in just a few days.

Daddy reasoned that he could do the same with the chemi-cals carried in Hobart's pest control truck. So he, Hobart and Ju-lius had set out to try this idea on a small stream out in Candler called Hominy Creek. Hominy Creek flowed past the American Enka Plant, a Dutch-owned Rayon manufacturing company started before World War II. They surmised that the stream was polluted anyway from the plant's emptying of chemical run-off and any fish they would kill would go unnoticed because they were always having fish kills.

Their experiment had turned out to be a success and no at-tention was paid to the dead fish remains they left behind, so it was concluded that they were ready to put the idea to anoth-er test. It was risky to attempt it on the first day of trout sea-son, but Daddy was closely applying the principle to the South American tribe in starting off the season with a bang. Hobart said he'd brought some termite pesticide the company no longer used, so he had plenty to use and none of it would be missed.

As it turned out, the river was teaming with trout and Daddy started the morning fishing regular. But the fish were just as smart as Daddy had said and they just weren't biting. It was as if they knew this was the first day of the season and they weren't ready to die yet. But that didn't suit Daddy, and he started get-ting impatient both with the fish and with Darrel and Hobart when he noticed how much they were drinking. Darrel and Hobart were a bad combination when Julius was not around and had started drinking as soon as they got together that morning. Julius was not there, due to a back problem caused by an old injury he'd sustained working on the railroad. This was a disappointment to Daddy and he was getting increasingly irritated with Darrel and Hobart. Daddy never drank liquor—never, and he never used foul language, because he always wanted to be in control and was educated and he said drinking and cussing made people stupid. Of course, he wasn't above breaking the law, but he viewed lawbreaking different from other people.

Daddy also never liked to come home with a small catch and, although he was catching a few trout, it wasn't enough to satisfy him. Darrel and Hobart were foolin' around and acting goofy and they weren't catching anything at all. Daddy decided to break them up and sent Hobart with part of the pest chemical to the far side of the river diagonally across and upstream from him and told him to pour in his portion of the chemical after he got there. He sent Darrel downstream of the pool to catch the overflow of raised fish while he poured in his measured portion into the water on his side of the river. But Hobart was too far away for Daddy to monitor and he'd had way too much to drink and forgot how much he was pouring in and poured some more and then some more and when the water flowed down and mixed with what Daddy had added, the river turned white and their plan backfired just as if the Great Forest Spirit had ordained it.

Daddy had calculated the termite chemical would only affect the river pool where they were fishing and boost up what they needed. But what happened next was almost unbelievable. The water was foaming white and the fish started coming up everywhere, at first like they was trying to breathe. Darrel and Hobart started scooping up the fish with nets as quickly as possible and then they all pitched in. Darrel used his hands to grab up a nine pound brown trout, the biggest one he'd ever caught.

But they couldn't gather them fast enough and the fish started dying and Daddy started yelling at everyone and blaming Hobart for the chemical he brought and they had to gather up the equipment and get out of there. The fish were streaming dead down the river beyond the pool and they just kept on dying and upending sideways with their eyes all bloated and staring. The water kept on flowing with dead fish by the hundreds as they headed out the gravel road and then down the mountain road toward the gateway, trying to make it to the highway before being noticed and keeping away from Hobart's van like it had nothing to do with them. They made it back to Asheville with no one chasing behind them and took Darrel home and unloaded the fish at his place and then drove the rest of the way home, not talking the whole way.

When they got home, Daddy told him not to say a word to anyone. When Momma came home from work later that day, Daddy told her they'd left the catch with Darrel for him to clean, explaining that they'd cut the fishing trip short because the fish weren't biting. After dinner that night, he overheard them talking about the evening news report, about how all the fish were killed all the way down the Davidson River, and how they'd overflowed the river banks in the town of Brevard, and how everybody was in an uproar because the first day of trout season was ruined. Daddy acted like he didn't know anything about it and told Momma it must have happened after they left.

The next few days there was lots more talk about the fish and there were stories in the newspapers about how the fish had been poisoned by the chemical Chloridane, which was four times as toxic as DDT, and how there was a major investigation in progress to find out how it got into the Davidson River. They didn't hear anything from Darrel or Hobart, and then something happened to upset everything. Daddy was reading the paper when he turned the page and there was Darrel's picture, as big as life. It was a photo of him with a big stupid grin on his face, holding up the nine-pound brown trout he had pulled out of the water with his hands.

Daddy went ballistic. It was a good thing Momma wasn't home because Daddy got as scary as a crazy man and started throwing things and stomping around like he could kill the first person he got hold of. The best thing anyone could do when he got like that was go hide somewhere until it was over. But when it was over, the coldness in him that followed was worse than the fit he'd taken. He brooded dark and solemn for weeks afterward. And when a State Game Warden named Steve Morrison came calling to question him about his whereabouts during the time of the river poisoning, Daddy told him to get off his property and refused to answer his questions.

Morrison had already been to see Darrel, who'd had the sense to get rid of the fish before the game warden got there, after Daddy threatened to kill him. Hobart had been smarter. After he'd made it back to Asheville that day, he'd unloaded the company van into a storeroom after handing in a finished work order for an exterior job he had supposedly done for a storage company on the other side of town. He'd picked that place as an alibi because he knew the owner and had keys to the gate lock for the regular servicing he did there. He'd returned there the next morning to leave evidence of the job he claimed to have done the day before.

When Darrel was questioned, he realized how stupid he had been and denied knowing anything about the poisoning and said he'd been fishing alone and had left the forest too early to have been involved. He held firm under intense pressure from Morrison because he would have rather faced jail than inform on Hobart or Daddy. At least in jail, he'd have a chance to grow older. So it ended up that no one was arrested because they didn't have enough evidence to prove they'd been involved. But that hadn't lessened Daddy's brooding rage. He'd become a suspect in what was now being called "The Davidson River Disaster" and had made a new enemy in Steve Morrison, who he knew would be a thorn in his side. Even Momma was suspicious now, but knew better than to say anything. Daddy was like a powder keg ready to go off for a long time after that.

CHAPTER EIGHT

"Let me sleep where I have lived—beyond the din of settlements."
— The last words of Natty Bumppo, by James Fenimore Cooper

What began the day of Morrison's visit to Robert's home continued until it became a long-standing feud. The Davidson River debacle faded into history for everyone but Morrison, the federal investigators he cooperated with, and Robert. It was always in the back of Robert's mind and his hatred for Morrison grew, far exceeding the resentment he'd harbored for Ranger Claude Austin. He was older and wiser now and had no intention of letting anyone get the best of him. He'd worked in intelligence during the war and knew how they operated, using spies and relentless pursuit to capture an enemy agent, no matter how long it took. He knew they'd never give up.

But he had his own powerful connections and influence with the back-end of the Buncombe County judicial system, friends who were lawyers and judges and Anne's boss, Bob Swain, who was probably his best "ace in the hole." That's how he'd found out the FBI was involved in the Davidson River investigation. He'd taken enough of his city hall buddies on clandestine hunting trips to expect a certain amount of loyalty from them and help when needed. Most of them were such hypocrites that they'd probably frowned with disapproval when hearing news of fish and game poaching offenses, and probably helped to prosecute offenders caught doing it. Some of them had clout, others had political ambitions, but none of them were elite enough to be invited to join the Biltmore Hunt Club so they were the first to go hunting with him when they could get the chance. And if they were raised in the mountains, even if they'd had certain advantages, they were still part of a mountain code of life that was older than the aristocratic society that barred their doors to those deemed not worthy of inclusion. Most of his friends were the sons of the old-time mountain politicians who made their own rules while doling out justice that made common sense to the people they served. And while this younger guard was rising to prominence and acted accordingly, they adhered to a deeper oath of allegiance that worked in everyone's favor. Robert was as much of a leader to them in the dark corner of their lives as they were to others in the light of day, because he served up adventure that took them away from their cluttered lives, heavy responsibilities, and the facade of respectability.

The fact that he cared for none of it and spit in the face of authority made them desire his kind of rogue independence because they knew they'd never have it. They were chained to the same behavioral restrictions as the people they represented and worked every day with offenders who broke every law of the land with abandon. Like the policemen who witnessed drug money changing hands in sums they'd never make in a lifetime of honorable service, members of the justice system witnessed examples of outrageous displays of freedom, and freedom taken away, that left them caught somewhere in the middle, making their lives seem at times a limbo of mundane entrapment.

The honorable few, like Robert's father-in-law, lived out their lives in benign respectability. Robert even gave him his due and knew that he'd married a woman he could trust and respect because of how she had been raised. But he'd been raised differently and couldn't help it and he lived by a set of principles that were governed by nature rather than man's laws. And he understood the nature of others like him and those who were weaker. He was a man formed by the wilderness and felt a kinship with it that no man could breach. And he would die defying anyone who denied him his right to it.

Ranger Steve Morrison was a more vindictive adversary than Claude Austin had ever been and he was in charge of a much larger territory. The Pisgah National Forest covered 510,119 acres of mountainous terrain, including the tracts of land purchased from the Vanderbilts that surrounded the city of Asheville and the French Broad Valley. The National Forest was divided into four Ranger Districts: the Grandfather, Appalachian, French Broad, and Pisgah districts. The French Broad Ranger District stretched along the Tennessee border from the Great Smoky Mountains National Park north to Hot Springs. The Appalachian Trail also passed through this section of the forest. Davidson River was one of three major streams and tributaries of the French Broad River located in the Pisgah Ranger District, which lay on either side of the mountain south of Asheville along the Pisgah Ridge. The Blue Ridge Parkway, under construction since 1936, would one day transect this National Forest with many of the forest and parkway trails intersecting.

It was a vast arena for a cat and mouse game between Robert and Morrison, and Robert had long experience in the game. It was second nature to him, the challenge of the hunter vs. the hunted, and sometimes, vice versa, as he well knew. It wasn't the possibility of being caught that had been aggravating him. It was the fact that Morrison had gotten the upper edge when Darrel had come under suspicion. Morrison knew that he and Darrel's father, Julius, were running buddies from way back and he probably knew about Hobart, too. Robert's history with the rangers had also been well-documented by Claude Austin. Morrison could set up a web of traps for him and put his rangers on alert in the forest. He could even try to predict his every move, but he couldn't make Robert his full-time job and he'd never completely understand what he was up against.

And so it was that another year went by while Robert focused on his riverboat business and kept his hunting activities within legal perimeters until things cooled down. And then one day in early autumn, without thinking, his impulses took over. It happened on a hunting trip he'd organized for his friends at Lake Mattamuskeet, located in the coastal area of the state that was part of his inspection territory. He'd gone to the lake to join

Bob Swain, Julius, who was now a bail bondsman, and lawyer friends, Tom Walton and Bruce Elmore, on a goose hunt. Lake Mattamuskeet was located in Hyde County and was North Carolina's largest natural lake, with an over 50,000 acre wildlife refuge known for its wintering populations of ducks, Canadian geese, snow geese and tundra swans. There were also concentrations of bald eagles and other raptors, wading birds and seasonal shorebirds. The North Carolina Wildlife Resource Commission regulated harvest of surplus animals to manage wildlife populations by issuing a limited amount of hunting permits. Prospective goose hunters applied for the September Canada goose hunt and Robert had arranged for his hunting party to lodge there for a week.

It was a week of hunting and drinking that was coming to an end. Robert, the only abstainer from alcohol, was up early the last morning and so was Tom. He and Robert went into the refuge to shoot geese as they returned from feeding. After shooting for a while, Robert left Tom with the geese and went for the car. He was walking on the shoulder of the road when a flock of geese flew low overhead. Although it was illegal to shoot from the road, the easy targets were too tempting for him to resist. He began shooting anyway without realizing that a State Game Warden was parked out of sight witnessing the whole thing. The warden's name was Calhoun and he wrote Robert a ticket.

Robert was more than furious and feigned ignorance, explaining that they'd been hunting all morning and he hadn't realized that he'd gone beyond the refuge. Calhoun refused to rescind the ticket, which only amounted to a $10.00 fine for violation of a local ordinance. Robert decided to ignore it and went back and got Tom and the geese and returned to Asheville. Communication between court jurisdictions from county to county was less than efficient during that time, but the State's game warden network was highly efficient in both communication and prosecutorial action, for even the most minor violations. When the fine was not paid and went into arrears, a warrant was issued for Robert's arrest and return to Hyde County where the refuge was located. This type of arrest warrant was valid throughout the state and a copy of it was sent to the Buncombe County Clerk of Courts where it went through the Office of the

District Attorney. But the warrant was flawed and Bob Swain promptly notified Robert about the warrant and that it wasn't valid because it failed to have the seal of the Clerk of Court of Hyde County on it.

The warrant was also in the hands of State Game Warden Steve Morrison who finally had a document that allowed him to legally pursue Robert. He and another game warden, Frank Spears, who was much older and had once been his senior officer, went to Robert's home to serve the warrant. Anne was home that day and invited them inside. She and Robert had known Frank Spears for years and they were on a first name basis. He'd been with the forest service much longer than Morrison and there had never been any bad blood between him and Robert. Anne insisted they sit down in the living room to wait while she called Robert, who was out back with Julius and Bobby.

When Robert entered the room with Julius close-by, followed by Bobby, he'd already been alerted to their presence and knew about the warrant. He acted relatively calm and let them know immediately that their warrant was no good. Morrison stood up and belligerently raised his voice, stating,

"The warrant is fair on its face and you are under arrest!"

Robert replied, speaking to both of them but looking directly at Morrison with a steady gaze of cold malice,

"Frank, you can stay, but *you*, Morrison, get out of my house, you're upsetting my wife."

Frank Spears, seeing that things were getting out of control and concerned about the warrant discrepancy, stood up and beseeched Morrison,

"Steve, go outside and wait in the car. I'll handle this."

Morrison ignored Spears and moved around the table toward Robert with the intention of putting him in handcuffs and arresting him. Anne was standing in the doorway of the kitchen looking to where Bobby was standing near Robert. When Morrison got to within arm's length of Robert, Robert swung his thick forearm around in such a slow lumbering movement that when it struck Morrison's jaw, the power behind it could be felt by everyone in the room. Blood splattered out of Morrison's mouth and his head slung backward and Robert started to pummel him with left and right punches that knocked Morrison to his knees. Morrison's gun fell to the floor from his unlatched holster as he slumped sideways toward the sofa trying to prop himself up with his elbows with no chance of being able to get into a defensive stance. Robert kept on punching left and right, left and right, with fists formed from huge ham hock sized hands, until Morrison swayed back and forth and then to the floor, his legs involuntarily jumping upward into the air and then plopping back down.

While Robert was beating Morrison bloody and unconscious, Spears made no attempt to intervene, except to pick up Morrison's gun from the floor. Anne made no sound and watched with mesmerized horror as her living room was turned into a boxing rink. Julius had pulled Bobby back from the fray but then stood with him as they watched the fight with fascination and excitement. The maelstrom that had spontaneously erupted in their midst left everyone who witnessed it astounded and shaken. Bobby had felt caught up in the action, drawn within the full force of his father's physical strength and merciless aggression. He'd seen blood before, but never splattered on his mother's curtains and living room furniture. He'd seen his father's anger, but never unleashed with such venom and velocity.

Spears held Morrison's gun in his hand but hesitated to use it for a variety of reasons, the primary one being the questionable validity of the warrant. Morrison was coming to and needed medical attention. Robert insisted that Morrison had been the aggressor and that he had acted in self-defense and in protection of his home and family. He even threatened to bring charges against Morrison. Spears warned him that there would be repercussions if he did so. He also warned Robert that the warrant, if invalid, would be corrected and reissued and they would be back to take him in. It was evident to everyone present that Spears had mixed feelings, and that he felt concern for Anne and Bobby. Anne seemed to be in a state of shock and the boy looked both traumatized and elated, a dangerous sign considering what he had witnessed. Spears also thought that none of it would have happened if Morrison hadn't been so heavy handed. He saw no reason to bring in local law enforcement, thinking it would only make matters worse. Instead he assisted the battered and nearly incoherent Morrison out of the house and into the State vehicle and took him to a local doctor for treatment, without reporting the incident.

Robert knew it wasn't over and that when Morrison recovered he would use his position to get back at him. Julius insisted that Morrison wouldn't press charges because to do so would shed light on his humiliating defeat, saying,

"You brought him down like a dog, man. And he'll bite your ass back like a dog as soon as he can move again."

As usual, Julius was impressed with Robert's ability to combat any situation without fear of retribution. Robert scared the hell out of him sometimes, but that's what made Julius look up to him, and had, since he'd been a boy. Robert had also used his influence to help Julius become a bail bondsman in Asheville, and a private investigator on the side. Julius knew that his occupation and sideline gave him access to information that was useful to Robert, but he didn't care. Robert had helped to elevate him from being mountain poor to being needed by socially upscale misanthropes who could not keep themselves out of trouble. Although it rankled that Robert associated with some of the upper echelon of the criminal justice system and called them friends, had even married the daughter of one of them, he understood why he did it. The difference between Julius and Robert was his acceptance of the fact that he would never be one of them no matter how many favors were exchanged or adventures provided. And while Robert's high-class friends might admire him, as he did, for his unbridled macho approach to life, they still thought of themselves as better, and therefore Julius held nothing but contempt for them.

Julius was fiercely loyal to Robert and filled an unofficial role as second in command of his underground network made up of relatives, barterers, moonshiners, whiskey runners, dealers, poachers, and every sort of illegal tradesman in their vicinity. And they all worked under the radar of a legal system riddled with corruption, a society that kept them in business, and a privileged few who benefited from all of them. Julius navigated this maze of complexity like a sailor who looks to the skies and the stars for direction. With his natural bent for espionage, he knew where to find every hidden cove and inlet of information to help his clients. He provided Robert with advice and the knowledge he accumulated in his bail bond business and private investigations. This gave Robert the leverage he needed when difficulties arose; Julius was one of the few people Robert would listen to. So it was Julius who convinced Robert to go straight to the hospital and be admitted for injuries sustained from Morrison before pressing charges.

The next day, Robert called Bob Swain from the hospital and told him what had happened. Then the two of them got together and met with the magistrate, who was also a friend and hunting buddy. The result was a warrant for Morrison's arrest on assault charges, claiming that Morrison assaulted Robert and broke Robert's finger with his jaw during an illegal attempt to arrest him with an invalid warrant. The magistrate went forward with the case and was about to give Morrison 30 days in jail for assault when a deal was struck to drop the Hyde County charges against Robert if he would drop his charges against Morrison.

After another humiliation, Morrison's animosity for Robert held no bounds and he swore that he would one day see him behind bars. Robert, on the other hand, remained silent but felt victorious and invincible and back in the game with a vengeance. The months he had spent hunting away from the Pisgah forest, trying to be cautious—which went against his grain—had yielded him nothing but problems. That forest was *his* territory and it was big, bigger than any of them, and he refused to be threatened away from it by Morrison or anyone else. So, he started poaching again, sometimes alone, and sometimes with others. Only this time he did it with more planning and forethought, avoiding the areas frequented by the state game wardens, the forestry service rangers, and the estate hunting parties. And he did this by accessing information, just as he had done when he was young. He not only relied on Julius and his underground resources, he put more effort into developing loyal friendships within the legal system by providing them with the stimulus they desired.

It was around this time that one of the attorneys introduced him to a man named Charlie Bradley. He wasn't a lawyer, was some kind of social worker, with caseload ties to the juvenile justice system and Robert's buddies at the courthouse. They called him CB and Robert took a liking to him after taking him hunting a few times. CB was big and friendly, and a charmer. He loved to hunt and fish more than anything and treated Robert with affability and respect. And he wasn't afraid to take chances, always asking to go with Robert whenever he could get away from his job. Like many of the weekend sportsmen Robert collected as friends, CB came equipped with the best hunting gear and attire the outfitter stores had to offer. And CB wore it well, was the picture of a modern-day sportsman; could have been on the cover of *Buck Hunters Magazine* or *Field and Stream*.

That was what set Robert apart from CB and the others he took with him on hunting trips. Robert didn't need all that gear; he had a Spartan approach to the hunt. He was a minimalist when it came to necessities. He rarely purchased anything new, repairing, retooling, innovating or inventing most of what he used. His rifle, shotgun, and hunting knife were kept in pristine condition and he reloaded his shells himself. He was a crack shot and lethal with his weapons. He was a superior hunter and woodsman on every level because he was born to it and raised to it and went through his rite of passage doing it, and moved through the forest like a native, like it was inherent in his blood.

He was something they could never be, and that was his hold on them because they knew when they were with him, they were in touch with something raw, primitive and basic. For some it was like sexual arousal, from their loins to their brains, overriding their fragile sensibilities that were being affronted on a daily basis in their civilized worlds. They were like men obsessed with a hobby, learning from a master, and even more than that, he influenced them to break the very laws they were supposed to uphold. And they did it willingly, and with an obligation to protect him from their system when called upon.

But why—why were these men drawn to a man who was nothing more than a criminal in the eyes of the law? What drew them into the forest, aroused in them a desire to hunt, to kill, to risk what they had worked so hard to attain? They were, for the most part, educated men, examples of success in American society, representatives of the law, cogs in the wheel of the legal system, serving several branches within an intricate and established hierarchy. And there, right outside their windows and doors, surrounding them as they traveled from their homes to their offices, from City Hall to courtrooms, from jail cells to

conferences, from cases to endless cases, they could see an en-
ticing panorama of mountains and wilderness just beyond their
reach, seductively shadowed in a blue velvet haze. It was a wild
and wonderful vista that wrapped its monumental arms around
their city as they scurried to and fro dealing with human crimes
and perversions, crisis and heartbreak, lawlessness and scan-
dals, penury and injustice.

And while many found comfort in their families, honorable
endeavors, social recognition, philanthropic activities, or ex-
tramarital affairs, those who were compelled to escape into an
embrace more compelling were susceptible to what Robert had
to offer because it promised something outside the norm, something that competed with their sober realities, tempting them to
break free from the reigns of conformity in order to experience
intoxicating boundless adventure.

It was a dream manufactured by stories most of them had read
growing up, images they had seen in their modern culture. It was
impossible for them to see the Blue Ridges of the Appalachian
range and not think of the days when frontiersmen roamed the
land. Frontiersmen like those immortalized by James Fenimore
Cooper, who in the 1820s created one of the most famous characters in American fiction. His hero, Natty Bumppo, also known
as Hawkeye, Leatherstockings and Pathfinder, was an American
knight, at home in the wilderness, who became the prototype for
future trappers and scouts, and later, the cowboy heroes, detec-
tives, and superheroes that dominated popular American fiction
and film during that time. The fact that this character lived on
and on in one form or another demonstrated the fascination that
continued to exist for such a man. Even early television during
the 1950s had their version of Davey Crockett and a song about
him that almost every school child could recite word for word.

Cooper himself had been a non-conformist, the son of a land
speculator who was raised in the frontier community of Cooper-
stown, New York. At age 13 he enrolled at Yale but was expelled
for blowing open a classmate's door with a charge of gunpowder
and roping a donkey onto a professor's chair. He went to sea to
find adventure and went on to become the author of the immor-
tal lone frontiersman. He was a rebel who created in his character an American creed that would later influence men such as

Ralph Waldo Emerson and Henry David Thoreau.

In Emerson's 1836 essay, "Nature," written at a time he was involved in a reformist group called *Transcendentalists*, he asserted that "God's presence is inherent in both humanity and nature and can be sensed through intuition rather than through reason." In his essay, "Self-Reliance" written in 1841, he called on his readers to strive for true individuality in the face of intense social pressures for conformity, writing that "Society everywhere is in conspiracy against the manhood of every one of its members. . . .Whoso would be a man must be a nonconformist."

Although these stories and essays were written over a century before, they had found a revival in the 1960s as a counterculture was railing against the Vietnam War and social norms. Women were asserting their rights and the Civil Rights movement was well underway. Never before had so many white men in America felt threatened, and in the South they had historically dealt with this through membership in secret societies that were now falling under severe criticism and scrutiny. Where better to go than deep into the forest, where a man could still be a man and learn to be self-reliant instead of being trapped in one cause or another, supporting issues that were only making him feel more infringed upon and vulnerable.

And then there was a man like Robert, a living representative of the lone frontiersman, who led them away from their concerns and gave them an example of a man who did as he pleased and got away with it. His followers were a chosen few, because each one had to be recommended by one of Roberts trusted allies and swear to an allegiance that could not be broken. It was a devil's pact, not a gentleman's agreement, and once they made it they were in for life. But it also became Robert's Achilles heel after the Morrison incident. He started to feel paranoid, that he needed more of an edge against his enemies, influential connections to counteract Morrison's influence with local law enforcement, and for that reason, he allowed CB to join them when in reality he knew very little about the man.

Robert even started inviting CB to the house, and over the next two years came to trust him like a brother. Bobby took a shine to CB, too, and as a result, that two year period of Bobby's life became the best he could remember. He would later use his memories of that time to block out the bad ones, the ones that woke him in the night and caused him to scream out loud. He held on to them for dear life because they were the only memories he had to remind him why he had loved and adored the father he came to fear and hate.

He often recalled them in sequence like a three act play:

Act One: Daddy had loved him then and had taken him everywhere whenever he wasn't in school. This had started soon after the fight with Morrison, the game warden, in Momma's kitchen. Daddy and Momma had started arguing a lot after that and things were upsetting at home. But Momma had no real power over Daddy. He'd gotten kind of sickly around that time and Daddy said he'd been coddled too much by Momma and Grandma Stanton. After an argument, Daddy would call to him, "Come on, son."

Then Daddy would say to Momma as he walked out the door, with him trailing behind, "You ought to know by now that it's my way or the highway."

They'd leave the house and sometimes be gone all day or all night. Daddy would put him on the flatboat and pilot it down the river past the estate private property signs and then to one of his trailheads where they would clear the underbrush hiding the trail. Daddy taught him how to sneak in and out and cover his tracks and recognize trail signs and watch the phases of the moon to know when to hunt at night. He learned how to trap and hunt and track and kill pheasant and grouse and wild turkey and other small game on the estate property. But nothing was like the day that he killed his first deer. His Daddy had held the 20 gauge, double-barreled shotgun with No. 3 buckshot and pointed, allowing him to aim and pull the trigger. A three point buck folded in the distance and the thrill of that moment came back every time he thought of it.

Act II: It was almost dark and very cold. It was so cold that Daddy had to keep the charcoal Hibachi fired up in the boat to keep them warm. There had been a heavy downpour the day before and the river was flowing high and rough. They were near the end of the float when they spotted rapids ahead. Daddy steered the boat to the bank, let him out, and told him to walk down the river's edge to a shore area where there was a big flat rock beyond the rapids; this was so he wouldn't drown in the frigid water if the boat turned over. He remembered tears welling in his eyes and trying to wipe them away as he watched his Daddy pull away from him and out into the rushing water, thinking all the while that he would never see him again and wondering how he would get back to Momma. But he did as he was told and made it to the flat rock and when he saw that Daddy had made it through the rapids, ran to meet him and jumped into the boat. Most of all, he remembered how good it felt when his Daddy, who was so big and strong and who could do almost anything, held him close the rest of the way.

Act III: They'd been spending more time with CB and he loved it when CB came with them hunting. Daddy seemed to relax in his company and these hunting trips were always special. Daddy acted different with CB than when he was with Julius or Darrel and Hobart. He was calmer, not ordering people around and getting angry because they were drinking too much. There was never any talk that made him feel creepy, like when he'd overhear things between Daddy and Hobart about hurting someone. When he was younger, he'd never worried about things going wrong, not until the fish got killed at the Davidson River. After that he worried all the time that things might get out of control, especially when Daddy brought Hobart and Darrel along. By the time he was 8 years old, he'd been able to figure things out from just a few bits of information by watching and listening. And although he knew that he was safe being his Daddy's boy, he still felt small and powerless whenever Hobart and Darrel were around. When CB was along, Hobart and Darrel were never invited. He never worried when CB was with him and Daddy. That was the best time, the best hunting trips, and the most good feeling he could ever remember.

* * *

That was how it was then, and so when Bobby was told by his father to do something that he didn't like, or something that frightened him, he did it anyway. Mostly he just watched things happen and listened at night when the voices downstairs got loud and he'd hear his mother crying. He was painfully aware that things had changed between his parents since the Davidson River fiasco, but not enough to prevent his mother from standing by his father, right or wrong. So Bobby believed that he should, too. His father was the whole world to him at that point in his life and CB had made Bobby look good in his father's eyes by the positive regard he showed for him whenever he visited in their home or when they went hunting together. Bobby loved CB for doing this.

Most of what Bobby learned about his father in the negative sense came from situations that erupted from his business dealings. It seemed that there were always problems. Robert didn't like to lose as much as a penny on a deal and was getting more tightfisted every day when it came to money. He'd been taught by Cora Belle to watch every cent when it came to dealing with people in the liquor business. Her teachings had carried over into every area of Robert's many enterprises. If he thought he'd been cheated, tricked, or falsely informed, he'd find some way to retaliate. If someone crossed him in any way, there would be a payback. Bobby overheard his father talking to Hobart about this on several occasions, and sometimes with Julius.

Julius was his father's oldest friend and he acted differently with him than with anyone else. He'd hear them talking about the old days when Robert would take Julius along with him on moonshine runs to help him load and unload the liquor. Julius would sometimes tell Bobby stories about his Dad, much to his delight.

"You should have seen me and him then, little Bob. I wasn't much older than you when we'd make those midnight runs. Man, did I hold on for dear life while your Daddy raced through the back roads of Buncombe County like the devil on fire. Hell, he'd outrun those revenuers and run through their traps like they wasn't there. They could never catch him because they didn't have the guts to take the road the way he did. Nobody drove like him and I can tell you that I was scared shitless the whole way."

What Julius didn't tell Bobby was how he'd sown his wild oats in the back rooms of illegal liquor houses where they delivered the moonshine and were serviced by the women there like young mountain kings. He'd idolized Robert then because he followed no rules and broke every law that got in his way. And nothing had changed between them except that the obstacles were more complicated, and the enemies more sophisticated, and the idolatry he once had for Robert had turned into fearful respect.

Robert had always been the leader, the older one in charge. Julius had spent his formative years mirroring him; his personality and beliefs had been shaped by Robert's influence. Julius was smart, but not as intelligent as Robert. He had a pleasant face and demeanor, but wasn't as good-looking and charismatic; he was clever, but not as diabolical, and not near as ruthless when angered. He'd grown up in Robert's shadow and had a significant role within it; he didn't know how to live otherwise. He was the favored one in Robert's extended family of scoundrels and held a position not unlike that of a mob family captain.

It bothered Julius that Robert was befriending and placing his trust in a man he hardly knew. This was unusual for Robert. The influence he had with his other white collar friends was based on an exchange of favors. And while, yes, he had eventually won their respect for his extraordinary abilities, they hadn't a clue to his true nature and criminal capacity. Julius, on the other hand, knew everything. And that gave him an edge with Robert as long as he maintained his trust. Julius was beginning to feel like he existed at the underbelly of Robert's life and CB on a higher level. Robert was spending more and more time with CB and less time with him. He didn't like it, but waited patiently for a chance to cast some doubt in Robert's mind about CB. So he started his own private investigation.

In the meantime, Bobby was floundering at school. He didn't really have any friends his own age at home and he'd missed a lot of school poaching with his father. Hunting was all he ever thought about. When he was in school, he felt different from the kids his own age, not connected; there were no shared interests. The closest person to him was his father, but he felt mixed up sometimes about where he fit in when his father's friends were around. Sometimes, his father was harsh to him, but never like he treated others. There were times when Bobby felt cocky. After all, he concluded, was he not his father's son? But he knew better than to test it. His father was a fearsome man and he'd seen him turn on people, and even though Bobby didn't think that he would turn on him, he didn't want to take any chances. It made him feel nervous just to think about it. The one person that made him feel safe, like he was really part of things, was CB. When CB was around, he didn't have to worry that something bad was going to happen.

That's why he loved it so much when CB came to the house or joined them on hunting trips. CB was a good man, like his Grandpa Stanton, Bobby could tell. He thought that his father must be a good man, too, if CB thought of him as a friend. His opinion of CB was based on the calmness and happiness he felt inside when CB was around. Maybe it was the man's kindness, and the way he would laugh so loud and hearty. His laughter could fill a room and change the atmosphere in it. His Dad rarely laughed, and when he did, it made people feel uneasy. His laughter was sometimes hurtful and mocking and made people feel foolish, stupid, inferior and ridiculous. His laughter could also be mean and cruel. But he never laughed at CB—never that way.

In Bobby's eyes, CB could hold his own with his Dad, and he wasn't afraid of anything either. He'd once seen CB shoot a wild pig that came at them right out of a scattering of blueberry bushes, charging like a small rhino, almost tearing into him before the bullet went into his brain and he went down. CB hadn't flinched for a second. Then there was the day that CB and his Dad had been out hunting the Pisgah high ridges when they'd heard the chilling cry of a panther. They'd found a slew of dead wild turkeys along the way and suspected the panther was ahead of them and probably aware of their presence. CB had refused to turn back when he was given the option, and didn't get spooked when the cries continued, echoing around them along the ridges, the scariest thing he'd ever heard.

His Dad had explained to CB how a panther or cougar will stalk by getting ahead of his prey, and then wait from a hidden vantage point until his target moved along the trail and then would follow and circle around to get ahead again to wait for a perfect time to attack, sometimes doing this several times while playing an unseen game with his prey. The panther must have decided that he didn't want to take on two men the size of his father and CB and took off on down the ridge. But it had been a close call. His Dad had even admitted it when CB told the story. But nothing seemed to faze CB, not copperhead or rattler, wild hog or cat, panther or bear; CB was a real man's man.

Well, there was one thing he was afraid of, bee stings. He'd never go near the honey bee colony that his Dad kept out back by the old barn. CB explained his fear of bees one evening when they were all sitting around the kitchen table after a dinner his mother had taken great pains to prepare. He told the story about how when he was a boy, he'd walked right into the middle of a bee swarm and before he knew it, he'd been bitten all over his body. CB had a way of making a story come alive. He described how his face and eyes had swollen up like a balloon because there was so much venom in him. He said he almost died right there and then.

"Ever since then," he said, "I've had a history of allergic reactions, the last one almost killing me again. It happened on a hot summer day while I was sitting in my office doing paperwork. My secretary opened a window in her office that didn't have a screen and a real determined bee flew right inside, turned the corner, and flew into my office like he was looking for me. The damn bee was buzzing around my head like he had a purpose in mind and when I tried to swat him away and called for my secretary to bring me a fly swatter, he dove at me like a Kamikaze pilot, just a grinning, like bees do, and taking great pleasure in stinging me where I sat. And just that sudden, my whole body began to react while I grabbed at that little buzzard and squashed him with my bare hand. But then my throat began to swell and my airways got all blocked up and I started wheezing and fluid filled my lungs and my heart beat faster and faster and I broke out in hives all over and my blood-pressure dropped and my pulse rate increased and my skin turned as blue as the mountain tops on a foggy morning.

"Luckily for me, my secretary thought I was having a heart attack and called 911. They almost misdiagnosed me because the bee sting symptoms faded quickly after I became unconscious. But then, one of the emergency nurses found the remains of that dead bee closed up in my fist and shot me full of epinephrine. She was a real looker, too," he winked at Bobby, "and she got me back on my feet in no time. Now I carry a kit with me just in case one of those little bastards comes my way."

CB could make anything sound exciting, even almost dying.

* * *

CB didn't realize what this revelation would cost him. Nor could he have known that Julius Cauble was working against him, stalking all around him like the panther had done that day on the Pisgah ridge.

Months went by before Julius, by pure chance, talked to someone who knew something about CB that shed light on his true character. Although CB was in an administrative position in the Department of Social Work, he had involved himself in a case that had stirred controversy because of the actions he had taken. The case concerned a family, a whole clan, dysfunctional to such a degree that a child had been taken from the home. The child, a little girl almost ten years old, had been found hiding in an abandoned trailer owned by a local resident who called the county Sheriff.

After she was hospitalized, examined and questioned, she was placed with child protective services and the court assigned a caseworker to investigate the home situation. The caseworker found it to be so appalling that she appealed to CB to aid in the permanent removal of the child from the home. The child had said nothing during questioning, but the examination had indicated repeated physical and sexual abuse. The caseworker suspected that she'd been sexually abused by her brothers, an uncle, and her father because she had not run to any of them for protection. CB became personally involved after reading her report and agreed to accompany her on a home visit.

In CB's view, the family was the worst example of mountain life: an enclave living in the backwoods, cutting themselves off from society, townsfolk, and condemnation. They grew their own food, welled their own water, killed their own game, and spawned their own mates, living in a clannish slum worse than any a city could foster in its worst tenements. They were ignorant and inbred and immersed in such poverty of mind and conditions that a child in that environment had little chance for escape from a bleak and dismal future. That she had tried at all was a testament to her courage.

The parents of the child had shown up in court looking almost civilized, denied the charges against them, and given sworn testimony that conditions in the home would improve. When it was decided that the child would be returned to the home after a recommended period of time in protective services, CB didn't explode in a rage, dispute the decision, or threaten the parents. He simply walked out of the courtroom and drove to the temporary safe-home where the child was being cared for, picked her up in his arms and took her away. It was not legal; it was not condoned by the office he represented, and it could have cost him his job if someone had informed on him. No one did. It was instead reported that she had run away again. The child virtually disappeared, her whereabouts unknown to both the family and the courts. A brief investigation followed but died out despite the family's outrage and threats to sue. They swore revenge and even planned it within the confines of their abysmal mountain compound, but couldn't get it together to carry out their scheme. CB had gone on as though he'd had no involvement, but people loyal to him knew that he did and rumor had it the child was placed in a secure and loving environment in another county. He was thought of as a man who was willing to act and accept the consequences for his actions when he felt that right was on his side.

Julius picked up this story nosing around in CB's business and listened to it with skepticism. It piqued him that, if the story was true, CB was heroic of nature. But then he found out more. He learned that CB was an environmentalist at heart and that his love of nature was equal to his desire to protect the innocent. He was a wildlife advocate who supported protection of the environment and he had close ties with the North Carolina Fish and Wildlife Services. Through a contact who worked as a janitor at the Pisgah Ranger Station near the Davidson River, Julius learned that there had been a series of meetings held there by the North Carolina Game Wardens and the FBI to form a cooperative effort in the ongoing investigation of the Davidson River poisoning. And he'd overheard talk of an informer who had infiltrated a group of poachers based in Buncombe County headed by a man named Robert Burris, who had been a suspect for years and had even been declared an outlaw for poaching the Biltmore Estate grounds.

Julius would have never found this out had he not been obsessed with the downfall of CB. He'd learned from experience that people in positions of wealth, power, and authority often pay little attention to their servants, suppliers, and maintenance workers. They sometimes forget that these people are typically local and come from families that have been in the area longer than they have. They cannot imagine the myriad links of communication that travel beneath their noses and how information spreads from mouth to ear and from family to family and from town to town. Julius found out that CB was an informer by talking to a cousin, who knew a friend, who worked with a janitor who cleaned up after the meetings at the ranger station. He'd gotten the job as janitor because he was willing to work nights, a second job after his day job, and took advantage of any hunting opportunity he could when his employers turned their backs because that's what he had been taught to do by his father.

The relatively new ruling class and offices of authority which ruled over the older mountain way of life was not met with outward rebellion; it would not have worked. Subversion crept through every nook and cranny of the mountains as quietly and pervasively as the green English ivy. And like the ivy, it grew without being noticed, disguised by flora and fauna and pine needles and tangled vines until it seemed to be everywhere.

When Julius told Robert what he'd learned about CB, he waited tentatively for his reaction with a mixture of satisfaction and apprehension. But Robert surprised him because he didn't react at all. He just stood there looking down at Julius, staring right through him as if he wasn't there. A chilling moment passed before Robert turned and walked away in silence, a trudging, deliberate stride with his head low-slung down, like Julius had once seen in an injured bear. But that bear had turned and attacked and Julius felt a shiver of fear run through his body such as he'd never felt before. He realized in that moment that he would not be thanked for the news he brought that day, but despised for it.

Bobby had no knowledge of any of this but he had been worried. He'd pushed the worry down like a squashed thought and tried to convince himself that his fears were imagined, that his father didn't really have it in for CB. So when they went fishing that morning, Bobby was excited and eager. It was just the three of them, what he liked the best. CB wasn't like the other men his father took fishing and hunting; they didn't want a kid tagging along. CB always acted pleased that Bobby was included, calling him "little man" and treating him like a big one. He bragged on Bobby's natural abilities and endurance and told Robert over and over that one day Bobby would be a great woodsman. Robert rarely praised Bobby and didn't comment when CB did. In every other way, he'd act friendly to CB, and at times, Bobby thought his father had gotten over his suspicions.

But that morning there was tight-wire tension in the air. CB didn't seem to notice it but Bobby did. He also thought it was strange that they were fishing legal in a permitted locale his Dad had once told him was worthless for catching trout. It was right near a logging road that accessed the forest through meadowland that would flood like a bog during the rainy seasons. Now he was telling CB that the trout would be running there and the catch good, despite the problems posed by the terrain, and that other fishermen were still avoiding the area because word hadn't gotten around about the improved conditions. Bobby tried to ignore the funny feeling in his stomach and thought everything would be okay because he was along, that surely his Dad wouldn't do anything to CB if he was there.

Bobby felt his father's escalation toward revenge as if he were part of him, living under his skin. He'd sensed the growing hatred and observed the insidious way his father disguised it in congenial companionable behavior. He had known that something would happen, that his father and CB were moving toward something bad because he'd lived with a foreboding of dread every day since the drive on I-40. But even with all the signs, with every indication that something terrible was going to happen, how could he foresee that he would be made an accomplice to murder? How could he imagine that his father would use him as an alibi, that he would rationalize what was about to happen as a life lesson for his son in the art of dealing with traitors? How could he know that CB's death would be like a line drawn down the before and after of his life?

CHAPTER NINE

*"If the tax-gatherer, or any other public officer, asks me, as one
has done, 'But what shall I do?' my answer is, "If you really want to do
anything, resign your office.' When the subject has refused allegiance, and
the officer has resigned his office, then the revolution is accomplished. But
even suppose blood should flow. Is there not a sort of blood shed when the
conscious is wounded? Through this wound a man's real manhood and
immortality flow out, and he bleeds to an everlasting death.
I see the blood flowing now."*
—Henry David Thoreau, On the Duty of Civil Disobedience

Bobby heard the shrill sound of a siren coming closer and louder and then heard car doors slamming shut and loud voices, and his father's distinctive one leading the others toward him and the body. The Sheriff's deputies and two ambulance men surrounded CB, one of them leaning over the body checking for vital signs. Then one of the deputies took his father off to the side where he couldn't hear what they were saying and the other deputy asked him what had happened and what he had seen. Bobby told them that CB fell over and they tried to save him but couldn't. The deputy looked straight at him, serious and stern, and asked him all about what they'd been doing before CB fell. Bobby felt sick and scared and tried to keep his face from showing anything and his stomach from throwing up his breakfast. Then he heard his father tell them,

"Leave the boy alone."

The body was taken away on a stretcher and they followed the deputies to the Sheriff's Department where Bobby was put in a room to wait and given a can of Pepsi to sip on. The cola helped to settle his stomach, but the pain in his heart would never go away, or at least that is what he believed. He thought he might as well have killed CB himself, seeing that he didn't do one thing to save him. He'd known it was going to happen and he saw it happen and he helped to drag CB to the hillside and he didn't do one thing to bring him back to life like they'd done the last time CB got stung. He'd seen his father rush up behind CB and grab his hand and slap that bee down on it with his gloved hand so hard the stinger went in right away. And then when CB was choking and gasping for breath and holding onto his father's jacket in a plea for help, he'd seen his Dad push him to the ground and lean over and take something from him that he slipped into his jacket pocket, and then stand there watching him while he struggled.

And all he'd been able to do while this was happening was stand there shaking and trying to see where CB's kit had gone because it wasn't on his belt, and thinking that it wouldn't make any difference because he wouldn't be allowed to help him even if it was there.

As Bobby sat there alone, feeling sick and heartbroken, he ruminated over the question: What can a boy do against a man? A man who sees someone coming to harm can fight the one causing it and protect the one who is being hurt. A group of people who are under the control of a leader, or a powerful group, doing wrong, can band together in strength to form a rebellion against the wrongdoers, like they do in a war; he'd learned that in school. But a boy with no one to help him and no friends to stand by his side, trying to fight a man like his Dad, had no chance. If he'd been carrying his own shotgun, could he have murdered his father to save CB? If he had thrown a rock, or pulled out his knife, it might have been like the David and Goliath story Grandma Stanton had read to him from the Bible. But he hadn't acted fast enough, and David had made a lucky shot anyway when he hit the giant Goliath. It was hard to always be accurate with a sling-shot even with lots of practice; besides, he hadn't had it with him anyway.

Bobby sat there in misery for over an hour and came to the conclusion that he had blood on his hands that would never wash off. He'd heard about such things, but couldn't remember where. Looking down at his hands, he envisioned them covered in red, the blood dripping from his fingers, the scent of it filling his nose, the sickening feeling churning in his stomach, and it was just as real to him as when he thought he'd seen the ghost of CB rising in the mist from the forest up into the clouds. He worried that the blood would be visible at night, preventing him from being able to sleep, reminding him of CB lying on the cold wet ground. And if he did go to sleep, it would probably be there in his dreams, but in them, the blood would be splattered everywhere, all over him and all over the house and even on his mother's living room curtains because he hadn't done anything to save his friend and he couldn't ever tell anyone about it. He had to hold the bad feeling inside and let it eat away at him — unless he could find a way to make it go away.

While Bobby waited, Robert's interview with the officers was becoming more contentious. He'd initially feigned co-oper-ation but stubbornly refused to go into detail about the death of his friend, other than to explain that he'd thought CB was hav-ing a heart attack and had tried to administer CPR to no avail. One of the deputies acted more suspicious than the other and this bothered Robert. He told them he knew nothing of CB's medical history and thought he was tough as nails. He even act-ed sorrowful to the best of his ability, and one of the officers had given him a sympathetic pat on the shoulder. But the other had eyed him all the way out the door, and he wondered if Bobby had said anything to make the deputy curious. He knew they had no evidence. And, he'd already thought of every angle and had gone so far as to take Bobby with them that morning just in case someone got the bright idea that this had been a planned execu-tion. Who would plan a murder and take a boy along?

When they got into the car to leave, he turned to Bobby and asked, "What did you say to the deputy who was talking to you?"

"Nothing, Daddy, except that we was going trout fishing and

CB fell down and died, that's all."

"Did you tell the man that I tried to help him?"

"No Daddy, he didn't ask me that. I didn't say nothin' Daddy, I promise."

Robert turned away from him and started the car. They drove all the way home in silence, both of them contemplating the deed that had been done. There would be no more conversation about it, but something had irrevocably changed between them. Robert had called Anne from the station to tell her about CB. After they got home, Bobby overheard Robert tell her that "the law was suspicious." Bobby wondered if he should be afraid, too.

The deputies came back several times to ask more questions over that next year, and then one day an investigator from the FBI came. After that, things really got bad. Robert started acting paranoid, thinking he was being followed, and the more he worried about it the worse he acted. But then, after a while, they stopped coming around and the pressure eased at home. However at school the pressure increased, because Bobby wasn't doing well, couldn't concentrate, felt different from his classmates, changed in some visible way. He thought he could never be like the other kids again, that he didn't fit in, was an outcast. He'd missed a lot of school and had become woefully behind in his studies and often didn't know what was going on. His grades kept slipping and it seemed that he had to work twice as hard as the others to keep from failing.

His teacher didn't help when she singled him out in class, asking questions that he couldn't possibly answer. His classmates laughed at him when she did this and began to jeer at him. He felt embarrassed and frustrated and began to act more defiant. The kids acted like they didn't want to have anything to do with him, and he made it worse by acting like he didn't care.

Most of the boys his age had bikes and he envied their ability to ride away to freedom instead of having to take the bus. And it bothered him that he wasn't growing as fast as some of them. His mother told him he would probably never be as tall as his father because he took after the Stanton side of the family, so he'd have to make up for it in other ways.

She must have said something to his father because the next thing he knew, he was enrolled in karate classes that were being given at the YMCA in Asheville. He was thrilled with the prospect of learning martial arts. And although he didn't know much about it when he started, he learned quickly and was praised by the instructor after only a few sessions. It was the first praise he'd heard since CB and was a balm to his spirit and a boost to his confidence. He began devoting himself completely to the art and practiced with discipline and regularity. This determined effort increased his stamina and released the natural inborn strength his Grandma Stanton had once told him he possessed. His instructor emphasized skill, mental focus, and quick reflexes as the advantage over size and bulk. These principles appealed to him greatly and for the first time in his life, he was beginning to feel a sense of power and control.

Karate took time away from schoolwork and Bobby's grades continued to plummet. Robert was an educated man and told him he didn't want an idiot for a son. He promised to buy him the English Racer bike he'd been asking for if he brought up his lowest grade of D-minus to a C. It was just the incentive Bobby needed to jumpstart his efforts at school. He continued his karate lessons with vigor and felt energized to work hard to bring up the grade. He blocked out everything else trying to cram facts into memory and written text into comprehension. He tried to listen and study but struggled to retain what he was learning. Concentration was still a problem, his thoughts invaded by unpleasant distractions. But he did improve and his hope and excitement increased to the extent that one night he dreamt of riding the bike, peddling so fast toward the edge of a ridge that he rode off into the wind and blue sky like a jet plane, circling the mountain peaks free as a bird. It was a wonderful dream, a dream to replace the nightmares, a dream he wished he could have again and again. But when the final test came, he scored a half-point too low, resulting in a D-plus instead of a C.

He remembered with agony the expression on his father's face when he showed him the report card, the slight grin of satisfaction. His Dad appeared to enjoy the fact that he didn't have to buy the bike, like he'd won some kind of bet. It was useless to beg or plead. It was the worst disappointment he'd ever felt and he couldn't let it go, couldn't accept that he'd been denied something he'd worked so hard to earn. Over the next several days his disappointment turned into anger; the extra half-point shouldn't have mattered, it was unfair, he'd been cheated, and it hurt so much he wanted to take it out on something or someone. Not his father, that was impossible. He'd never felt such meanness inside; he tried to direct it into karate, like he'd been taught by his instructor. As far as school was concerned, he didn't give a damn anymore. Learning to fight was more important and martial art skills would make him tougher. It was something no one could take away from him.

He came to this notion by a process of self-taught self-assessment born out of frustration and despair. In just a short time, the practice of karate had taught him that he could have some control in a world where he'd had none. He was like a fledgling trying his wings, testing it out with defiance and rebellion toward the teacher and the kids at the school, testing it with his mother at home, and it was beginning to work because they didn't know how to handle the change in him and they all started to back off. The only problem was that he miscalculated this newly acquired sensation of power in relation to his father. The day that CB died had changed his life forever, but the worst day of his life was about to happen, one he would never forget.

It was a cold autumn morning and his Dad had gotten him up early to go down the river duck hunting. They hadn't been hunting since the bike episode, the loss of it still bothering him. The river was running smooth and steady but his actions were slow and surly. His attitude was ignored, which made his disposition worsen because he wanted his father to know how he felt. They were in a flat-bottom boat floating down the French Broad to the place where the river widened and the wild ducks gathered. A yellow rim of sunlight cut through the grayness of dawn and the forest came alive with sounds of creatures awakening to a new day, a perfect day for shooting. But the enthusiasm he usually had for duck hunting was gone and it showed. He'd never acted like this with his father before and knew he was playing with dynamite, but couldn't stop himself. His cocky behavior of late was getting harder to contain and he thought he had a right to air his grievance once and for all.

His father finally paid attention and said, "What's your problem, boy?"

It came out as a sudden outburst, "Why can't I have the bike, Daddy? You can afford it and the other boys all have one, and I did almost make that grade."

"Because you don't need it!"

"But I do need it, and you promised."

"You didn't make it, boy. Almost making it isn't making it."

"You're glad you didn't have to buy it."

His father glared at him in response.

He should have stopped right then, but couldn't. He just couldn't. It spewed out of him, like vomit does when a person suddenly has to throw up,

"Maybe I'll tell what we did to CB . . .

The swift motion caught him by surprise and took his breath away. The next thing he knew was being held upside-down by the ankles over the rim of the boat. He remembered looking down at the water and smelling it—the odor of fish and frogs and dank leaves—feeling it lapping at his hair, the frigid temperature freezing his head like an ice cap. The 20 gauge shotgun shells that he'd filled his pockets with that morning emptied from his jacket falling past his ears bloomp, bloomp, and bloomping into the current. The river kept on flowing while he remained suspended, held in the grip of his father's unforgiving hands and hearing his voice filled with hatred and rage,

"You think you can turn on me, boy? I'll drown you right here, right now. I'll tell everyone that you fell in, and your mother will support me."

"Please Daddy, please. Don't drown me Daddy, please."

Time stood still as his mind raced. The mental focus that he'd been trying so hard to master and the skills he'd been working so hard to attain were worthless against this man. The mighty river that his father had once protected him from by putting him on the shore could now be his grave; the power to save him or kill him was held in those big strong hands; they had all the power and always would. And no matter how loud he screamed and cried and begged and squirmed as his life was held in the balance, a line had been crossed with his father and he knew what that meant. He was in a state of stark terror, not because he thought that his Daddy might kill him, but because he believed he would.

And then it was over, as swiftly as it had begun, and he lay in the corner of the boat where he'd been thrown, crying and shivering. There was no comfort extended. He would never again be held in the arms of his father as they floated down the river. He would never again feel that he was "*his* boy" special from the rest. The bond they had once had was severed completely and he would never again feel any level of security. A harsh reality hit him like a thunderbolt: the realization that he was expendable, just like CB had been.

The burgeoning self-assurance he'd been developing since taking his karate lessons was shattered into pieces. And just as before, he'd have to deal with the fear and loss alone; a loss that was harder to take because he felt rejected and abandoned and couldn't talk to anyone about it. Now more than ever, he understood the grim consequences of betrayal. In his mind, there was no escaping the lot of his life. He was only a boy—just a boy. But by the time his sobbing stopped, the self-protective shell that would form over his young heart and troubled conscience had already begun to harden.

CHAPTER TEN

*People talk sometimes of a bestial cruelty, but that's a great
injustice and insult to the beasts; a beast can never be so cruel as a man,
so artistically cruel. The tiger only tears and gnaws, that's all he can do.
He would never think of nailing people by the ears,
even if he were able to do it.*
— *Fyodor Dostoyevsky*, The Brothers Karamazov

Bobby had grown in size and strength since that day on the
boat and was now adept in the practice of martial arts. In many
ways developing the skills had been his salvation but also his
curse. By sticking with it after everything else in his life had
seemed to fall apart, he'd regained a semblance of self-respect
and it showed in his attitude and behavior. At school he carried a chip on his shoulder and projected a tough exterior that
generated an air of tension which had an intimidating effect on
others his age. He was no longer in elementary school. At the
Sand Hill Jr. High School, he'd gained a bad reputation and a
group of friends that fostered it. He did the minimal to get by in
school because there was no alternative. His father controlled
his life and complete failure was unacceptable. There were no
more incentives for good grades; he wouldn't have trusted them
anyway. He did what was necessary to pass, looking forward to

the day it would all be over and he would be out from under his father's rule.

His childhood had ended that day on the French Broad River, and the young man that emerged from the ruins of his boyhood was still dependent on his father. Their relationship was rebuilt on a foundation of wariness and mistrust. It started with a series of orders given to test him, to see if he would try to rebel again. He'd be told to do chores that he'd never been expected to do before. And if he didn't finish them, he'd be made to stay out until after dark until they were done. Then, additional chores would be added on. If his mother tried to ease the burden by helping him and his father found out, there would be an argument. When she tried to stand up to him, he would belittle her and say,

"It's for the boy's own good."

Bobby accepted the punishment and continued to obey and after a while his father let up and they started hunting together again. There existed a strain between them that lessened when they hunted; he'd learned that the hunt took precedence over everything, particularly if risk-taking was involved. But he didn't realize that he would continue to be tested over the next several years.

It really began when Bobby was 12 years old. Robert started the tradition of taking him on hunting trips to the North Carolina coast over the Christmas holidays. The common bond they now shared was disrespect for the law, poaching new territories, and pushing the limits of authority. This was the third of these trips and they were off to Hyde County, the same county where Robert had gotten into trouble at Mattamuskeet Lake. It was typical of him to return to a place that had given him trouble; to traverse an area where he had been forbidden to roam was a challenge he couldn't resist.

Robert was still determined to hunt where he wanted to, follow his own rules, hunt on private land if the game was there, and outwit anyone who tried to stop him. Throughout the year, he traveled to the coast regularly as part of his job and always took time out to scout new hunting sites whenever he had the opportunity so they would have several options. The private land where they had hunted the year before was the first stop they made on their way down the coast.

After they checked into a motel and had dinner, they waited until dark before setting off on foot with their two-way radios, guns, silencers and spotlights. The fairly isolated motel had been chosen because it was situated near the property where they were headed. The motel was located three miles off the interstate and banked on one side by a parcel of land that was surrounded by an enormous maze of swampland called the Great Dismal Swamp that remained undeveloped. According to their map, the adjacent private property, a mile down on the other side of the road, consisted of 40 acres of farm and forestland that was easily accessed from the motel.

When they reached the private property and crossed over onto it, they began checking out the terrain. They even moved up close to the landowner's farmhouse where they found a set-up to lure deer: salt licks and a duck pond surrounded by a forested area. A swamp buggy used for land or water was parked by the pond. It made a perfect hiding place to watch for the deer if they ventured out from the forest edge. Robert told Bobby to hide there while he crept silently toward the pines to see if he could spook one of them.

The plan worked like a charm when a large five-point white tail buck leaped into the clearing and stood paralyzed by the spotlight. Bobby aimed and was about to fire when a light came on in the farmhouse and a man started shouting from a window that he was going to call the sheriff. He ran from behind the buggy toward the forest where Robert was waiting and they took off into the woods and up onto a ridge where they were able to look back down and see the outside lights come on and the man come outside with his shotgun. They stayed put, quiet and unseen in the darkness, and watched until a sheriff's deputy arrived and did a cursory search of the area surrounding the farmhouse while the man kept harassing him to search farther into the forest.

After the deputy left, they headed back to the motel, staying far enough from the road to be safe, and then settled back into their room for the night. The next day they drove to the coast and obtained fishing and hunting licenses, something Robert always did to maintain a legitimate cover, and spent the next few days fishing the coastal waters and hunting on state lands. It ended up being one of the only legitimate trips they had made. But on the way back up the interstate, as they neared the motel exit and the troublesome landowner's property, it was sticking in Robert's craw that the man had gotten the best of him. Robert was not about to let it go and pulled off of the exit. When he re-checked them into the motel for the night, he said to Bobby, "We're going to get that bastard."

Bobby replied, "What do you want me to do?"

Later that night, when they snuck onto the landowner's property and near the farmhouse, Robert handed Bobby the hatchet he'd taken from the trunk of the car, his Bowie knife, and a two-way radio, telling him he would stand lookout. Bobby attached the knife to his belt and slipped the radio into his jacket pocket, and with the hatchet held in a tight grip, crouched low and moved like a spider across the clearing to the swamp buggy. He used the sharpened hatchet to cut open the tires and the knife to cut the wiring harnesses and seats and did as much damage as he could do to the vehicle in the time allotted. Robert radioed Bobby that the coast was clear and he ran upright back across the clearing and reported what he'd accomplished.

Bobby was exhilarated by the mission and overcome with happiness when Robert gave him a nod of approval, indicating his satisfaction. When they made it back to the motel, Robert fell into an exhausted sleep, but Bobby lay awake reliving the experience and the intense pleasure he'd felt having done something right for a change. He was no longer his father's reject, his beast of burden, his slave. He had graduated to another level, was an accomplice, and that made him almost an equal, almost.

The following fall Bobby entered Enka High School. There he found an even bigger pool of misfits than were in middle school and they gravitated toward him like moths to a flame. They admired him because he didn't care that the decent kids at school wanted nothing to do with him. They also hung around him because they were in great jeopardy as unpopular freshmen, picked on by older bigger football players, and drilled daily by the high school coach, who saw them as losers. They admired Bobby because he had more guts than they did and acted like a leader to them.

Their most formidable antagonist was Coach Moore. Coach Moore had noticed Bobby's influence over his friends and zeroed in on him. His efforts to get Bobby to participate during gym sessions were met with resistance. Moore started making an example of him and his friends, ordering them to run laps around the gym, humiliating them in front of the other students, who sat and laughed at them without being reprimanded.

One day after one of these episodes, Bobby and the other students from gym class were waiting outside to begin practice on the athletic field when he noticed Coach Moore's truck parked nearby in the school parking lot. The idea struck him immediately and he knew exactly what to do, what his father would do if he'd been subjected to such maltreatment. He eased away from the others until he was out of their line of vision and then crouched low once he reached the parked vehicles in the lot, using them for cover until he made it to the coach's pick-up. He swiftly pulled out the knife he always carried and plunged it into the two tires on the passenger side in several quick successive motions.

The hissing sound that came from the tires was louder than he had expected. The slashes were not deep enough to let the air escape quickly, creating a seeping noise that sounded like a whistle as the air pressure from inside the tires forced its way out. Bobby moved away from the pick-up, intent on hurrying back to join the others. He was relieved to see that they were headed in the direction of the field and that their focus of attention was distracted away from him. His walk almost turned into a run as he scurried around the other vehicles and away from the scene and the escaping air that he could almost feel whooshing behind him.

At that very moment, the assistant coach came out of the side door of the gym to retrieve a box of new sports equipment from his car that was parked near the coach's truck. He noticed Bobby moving through the parking lot in a furtive manner, heard the diminishing sound of the air escaping from the tires, saw the coach's truck tilt to one side and immediately made the connection. He yelled to Bobby, ordering him to stop in his tracks. Bobby turned, startled as an immobilized deer. The assistant coach caught up with him and grabbed his arm roughly. There were no questions asked as he was practically dragged to the principal's office.

Bobby had been taught to never admit to anything so he denied cutting the tires and continued to deny it under the stern denouncement of the principal. His mother and the Sheriff's Department were notified and a deputy was sent to the school to pick him up. He was unceremoniously led down the hall in front of all of the students who were changing classes and out the door where he could be seen by the gym class leaving the practice field. Bobby felt scared and embarrassed and it seemed as though a thousand eyes were staring at him from every direction. He was taken to the county juvenile detention center. His mother arrived shortly thereafter and made arrangements to pay the damages. He was released into her custody and also suspended from school for a week.

At home, he waited with apprehension for his father to come home, the one person he thought would understand and quite possibly praise him for his actions. Instead, his father came home in a fury, looked at him with disdain, and ridiculed him for cutting the tires in daylight with so many people around and for being so careless and impulsive. When Bobby tried to defend himself by referring to the swamp buggy incident, his father replied, "I didn't tell you to do anything like that to a coach!"

Bobby soon realized that he was not being berated for the wrongdoing of his actions, but for being stupid enough to get caught. And the punishment his father thought up for him was, in Bobby's thinking, beyond cruel and unusual; it was completely unjust and unfair. In later years, he came to view it as another milestone in his life, the memory a reoccurring reminder of when he lost his soul to darkness:

It began early the next morning following the day of his suspension from school. His father had left before dawn to attend a farm auction near Asheville and returned hauling a 14-foot tractor he'd bought for a pittance. It was covered in rust and looked as if it belonged in a junkyard. His father unloaded it from the flatbed trailer into the middle of their cornfield and then, before leaving again for work, ordered him out to the field to begin what he called a "restoration project" on the tractor, which he took to mean his punishment and rehabilitation. It was a bitterly cold day and he didn't have sufficient clothing for the weather. He rarely had the right clothes for anything because his Dad was so cheap he and his mother often went without the bare essentials. His work gloves weren't the right size and he'd been handed a box of old sandpaper and scrapers and tools and expected to do a job that was impossible; he didn't have a clue where to begin or how to go about it. He was told that he could not leave the job for any reason until it was inspected at the end of the day.

He started scraping, making little progress as his hands became frozen numb from the cold. After a while, he did it by rote to keep himself from freezing and being overwrought with the injustice of his punishment. There had been no intervention from his mother. She didn't even try. He knew she was as powerless as he was, but it hurt him just the same. She didn't even visit his grandparents much anymore. They were getting old and didn't understand anything about her life. He'd felt ashamed to see them, too. He loved Grandma and Grandpa Stanton, but they could never know about the things he had done and it was easier if they couldn't see the change in him. He was not their grandbaby anymore: the boy they thought was so smart and funny, so sweet-natured and good, his grandmother's little heathen, who delighted in bringing her presents from the woods.

Grandma Stanton would talk about God's love and the Bible and sing hymns she'd learned at church that she taught to him. He tried to remember one of them, the one about having a friend in Jesus, but the words wouldn't come. It didn't matter. Jesus would never want to be his friend and God was probably downright mad at him. After he'd helped murder CB by not trying to save him, no one as good as Grandma or Jesus or God would want anything to do with him. It was useless to even think about it or pray for help. That was probably why his parents didn't go to church. They were past help and so was he. But still, something inside of him cried out as the day wore on and there was no relief from the icy wind and the dismal gray sky that hung over him like a massive oppressive cloud,

"Oh God, please help me anyway, please."

His plea was met with silence and he stopped to stare at the house in the distance, noticing that his father's car was coming up the driveway. He wondered how long it would take before he came out to the field to inspect his work, and after an endless period of time passed, he wondered if he was being watched from the kitchen window and continued scraping, praying for it to end soon, for the punishment to be over. But when he did come out, his father was unforgiving as he looked at the large section of rust that had been removed and ordered him to return to the field the next day and then the next, and when it was finally over, he'd stopped praying for help and started hating his father for the hypocrite he was, and hating himself for trying so hard to please him.

The next week he'd returned to school and found another type of hell waiting for him there. The word had gotten around about what he had done and he was treated like vermin by the teachers and most of the students. The athletes on the football team were the worst, singling him out as their favorite target, picking on him relentlessly. They were much bigger and older and it didn't matter to them that he was only a freshman. There was one in particular by the name of Jake Ransom, who took exceptional pleasure in knocking him into the hallway lockers, calling him filthy names, and cornering him whenever he got the chance. A few of his friends remained loyal and hung out with him knowing they would suffer similar abuse. The others were too afraid to stand by him and he wouldn't forget their disloyalty.

There were days when he thought it was too much to bear and then one day, as if out of nowhere, an old saying he'd heard somewhere popped into his mind, "the straw that broke the camel's back" and the meaning of it began to develop great importance to him. With each incident and every offense to his person and sensibilities, his response was to accept it like another straw and then another that was piling up on him in preparation for what was to come. As it built momentum in his mind, piling up high and weighty, he carried the burden each day with greater intensity of thought and determination. He practiced karate at night in his bedroom and performed physical labor at home with eager acceptance, driven by hatred and the desire for revenge. He ate when he wasn't hungry and worked when he wanted to rest. As the months passed by, he visualized the pile of straw growing in size and density as his own size and bulk and strength increased to carry it. It was like preparing for a martial arts competition in the way he'd been taught by his karate instructor. He could either be crushed by the tyrannical force of his opponent or overcome the odds by gaining strength of mind, body and spirit, by thinking like a warrior instead of a slave.

The day of the final straw began like any other. But this time when Ransom knocked his books from his arms and slammed him into his locker, knocking his head against it, the straw broke. In that instant, he turned around in a flash using every move he had practiced and then leaped on Ransom like a tiger, beating him with flying fists of rage and with such rapid fury that Ransom tried to retreat and fell backwards and he'd held on and punched him about the head until he heard the groans of agony and saw the blood of victory and went in for the kill, stopping himself short of it by using the discipline he'd learned in karate, having defeated his opponent with skills more suited to a "no rules barred" street fight. His audience of students had watched in amazement, backing off and crowding around at a safe distance, not one of them trying to intervene. It was over so fast that the teachers were not alerted and he'd walked away unscathed and gone to class, leaving his victim humiliated and left to lick his wounds. No one reported the incident.

From that day forward, everything changed. The jocks quit bothering him and he was treated with more respect from the other students. He knew he would never live down what he'd done to the coach's tires, but in high school there were other outcasts and they were growing in number and less attention was paid to him because he was no longer a problem. He'd found his dignity and within it would find his way to the end of the road there, gathering followers along the way, most of whom lived in trailers and came from homes much worse than his, who looked to him for direction, and became his first real gang.

In school, he kept a low profile, improved his demeanor, and continued to make barely passing grades. He was treated as if he had a learning disability and basically ignored by the teachers who found it easier to just pass him on. He believed it to some degree, but also trusted his basic intelligence, his instincts. He knew that he couldn't learn much at school because he had trouble concentrating there and felt insecure when it came to schoolwork. But away from school, when he was outdoors, his concentration was acute and he could teach himself what he thought was important to know.

As he began to see the different effect each of these situations had on him, he learned the value of staying out of the spotlight at home and at school, to "cool it" when around adults and give the appearance of playing their game. In the forest, he felt confident in his ability to analyze situations and plan strategies. He met with his friends away from the school grounds and limited his association with them during school hours. He didn't want to be seen as a gang leader because it created too much attention; he found secrecy a more compelling idea for his future. He planned extracurricular activities in the forest, calculating times and locations that would keep him under the radar of his father, taking advantage of his absences, when he was away at work or on hunting trips.

The most important thing he had come to understand was the power of violence. Violence had made up for all of his inadequacies, had broken him free and changed his life for the better. The explosion of it, triggered by Ransom, had actually calmed him and helped him to cultivate restraint, to keep his anger held at bay while he continued to hone his skills. He visualized his violence as a snake peacefully coiled inside of him, ready to strike if prodded.

An added benefit to his persona had been occurring naturally since puberty; his voice had changed dramatically taking on a deep resonant tone, a genetic gift inherited from his father. It gave him a surprising edge over his companions who, for the most part, still sounded like boys. The friends he chose to lead were made up of an assortment of characters who appealed to him for one reason or another, the main one being that they allowed him to be in charge. But there was one area in which he lacked experience and worried that it might be taken as a sign of weakness. His friends wanted to drink alcohol when they got together and some of them had been drinking for years whenever they could get it. None of them had money to buy it and it was too easy to get caught if they tried to steal it. So, they appealed to him to solve the problem.

He'd been brought up to disdain liquor and had been shown

examples of what it did to people when they got drunk. His father had an aversion to alcohol that bordered on obsession and yet he always kept it stockpiled for use in bartering or bribing or supplying his buddies and their friends. It was like forbidden fruit stored in their root cellar, something he couldn't have but began to desire in an effort to impress and appease his own friends.

His father was a hoarder and always kept a stash of moonshine and assorted goods hidden away, but he also had an uncanny ability to keep track of his merchandise and could tell if even one item was missing. It wasn't long before he noticed that some of the full moonshine jars were gone. When his Dad questioned him about it, he denied any knowledge. Since he'd never been in trouble for drinking or showed any indication of inebriation when around his parents, he was given a temporary reprieve from further inquisition. He was smart enough to know that he wouldn't get by with it a second time, so he changed his tactics and considered an alternative source.

Most of his gang lived on the outskirts of Asheville, as he did, except for Johnny McCabe, who was probably his closest friend. Johnny lived in the backwoods with his widowed father in a rough-hewn cabin that had been built a century before. They were as poor as the dirt that shaped the rocky hollow enclosing their humble dwelling, but rich in one important area, as far as he was concerned; Daddy McCabe was a moonshiner. McCabe rarely left his homestead and depended on Johnny to deliver his goods when they couldn't be picked up. But Johnny had to account for every jar and every cent and Daddy McCabe was wily as a fox when it came to his still and his product.

Johnny was the youngest of the gang, only 14, but tall as a beanpole, red-headed, rangy, good-natured, near-sighted, and a little crazy. Once Johnny heard the idea, he agreed to tell his father about a new customer who was willing to trade fresh game for moonshine. Johnny laughed when he reported back about how his Daddy's eyes lit up at the prospect cause his eyesight had been going, his shooting aim had been off, and his hunting days were about over, so they hadn't had much in the way of meat or fowl on the table. Johnny couldn't hit a target if it was placed right in front of him and since his mother had passed, the only good meals they'd had were when they had fresh game to roast.

The deal with Daddy McCabe was made. Alcohol was now available but could only be attained by poaching. He'd poached with his father long enough to know every trail and entry point onto the estate grounds and how and when to do it without getting caught. He chose Johnny McCabe, who had many skills but couldn't shoot worth a damn, and Ernie Justice, who could, to accompany him on poaching raids using his Dad's flatboat, which he had learned to poll down river to the estate grounds. They could only manage to take this risk about once a month when his father was away, but even so, they kept Daddy Mc-Cabe supplied with game and Johnny came back in return with the moonshine.

For Bobby it had been like the discovery of a magic elixir. He loved the burning sensation in his throat when he swallowed the honey-smooth fluid and the warm feeling it generated as it flooded into his bloodstream. It set his imagination on fire and dispersed all his anxieties, replacing them with a feeling of ex-hilaration and invincibility. It sometimes spurred his aggression, so he drank only when in the forest, where it could be expressed in a multitude of ways, where he could impress his friends with his daring, lead them into fearless adventure, unleash his pent-up hostility, and feel the ultimate sense of freedom. Alcohol en-hanced every sensation and he craved the intoxication and deliv-erance it gave him.

He felt better about everything when drinking, but also felt okay when not drinking. Sometimes he drank too much, but his youth, health, and vigor deflected most of the negative ef-fects from his excessive bouts of alcohol consumption. He re-alized that he had a tendency to overdo and that he needed to maintain control of himself at home and at school. There were times when he became combative and mean when drinking. His friends didn't like it and he didn't like losing their respect, so he tried to limit his intake, and was fairly successful, for a while. The utmost reason he had to be cautious with alcohol was fear that his father might find out and that was the most sobering incentive of all.

There was also a girl, his first real girlfriend. He had been with other girls and had sexual experiences with some of them, the ones who looked for trouble, skirted the perimeters of popularity at school—girls who would go into the woods with him or any other member of his gang. He'd experimented freely when the opportunity arose, sometimes prompted by his friends, but he wasn't bent that way, never had been. There was something he remembered in the loving gentility of his Grandmother Stanton and her strength of character that produced a yearning in him for those qualities in a girl, and the desire for it was there in the earliest throes of his puberty, without his full awareness. He'd seen fragments of it in his mother, and he often fantasized about the way she must have been before being lost in the clutches of his father. He'd seen a photograph of her at his grandparents' home on the mantel. She was dressed in a white lace dress with a string of pearls around her neck and a loose bouquet of gardenias draped across her lap, her golden hair waving down to her shoulders, her head held high. That was the image that stirred him.

But his mother's strength had been beaten down and her gentle nature hardened, and she had not been able to protect her only son, nor herself. So the ideal of his fantasy, which grew from this deprivation, combined softness and strength, gentleness and bravery, was nurturing and protective, beautiful and daring, and these qualities formulated within him into a sensual desire that both stimulated and soothed him, a balm that erased the abuses he had suffered and the brutality he'd known and engaged in. The desire was not merely sexual but an all-consuming need that could be triggered by just one or two of these attributes.

Kristy McFarland possessed several. He'd known Kristy since middle school. She was one of those girls who was nice to everyone, had been friendly to him when everyone else was looking at him with scorn. She was feminine and pretty without acting like she knew it, tall and athletic and participated in sports on the girls' soccer team. He'd kept his distance, believing he hadn't a chance with her, fearing that she might reject him because of his reputation. But things had changed since the slashed tire incident. They'd both matured physically, and alcohol was the great equalizer that gave him the courage to pursue her. When she responded with genuine affection and let him know that she had been attracted to him all along, he fell hard. She was sweet and reassuring, had a soft voice and easy laugh. Although she was as tall as he was, she made him feel big and strong. She seemed to care little about his past, looking only for the best in him, complimenting him on his sense of humor, and telling him how much she loved his deep voice. With her he felt special, and even tried to be funny.

Time spent with his gang was kept separate from his time with Kristy, like two different worlds and two different sets of behavior. He didn't want her around them. She was wholesome and pure, had soft chestnut brown hair, big brown innocent eyes, a tender heart and a body ripe and responsive. He wanted to keep her safe from harm and from too much knowledge about his life. He invented a better one for her that spared her from the problems he dealt with every day at home. He was able to pull this off because he didn't take her there. It helped that she wasn't permitted to go out at night during the week and their time together was limited to an hour each day after school and longer periods on weekends.

Bobby began to hope for a future with Kristy and agreed to meet her parents. She came from a good family, he could tell by the way she talked about her parents; their home life seemed secure and stable. But he was nervous about meeting them and was determined to be on his best behavior—mannerly, polite and respectful. Her mother and father were hospitable and kind to him. He could see a little of Kristy in each of them. Her father worked at the Ecusta Paper Mill in Transylvania County and her mother worked at Southern Bell Telephone Company. Their home was modest but comfortable, nicely decorated, warm and inviting. He imagined that her bedroom had ruffles on the curtains and tiny roses on the wallpaper. They had home-cooked meals every night of the week even though both of her parents worked, and Kristy always helped her mother with the dishes. She had a strict curfew that she willingly adhered to and didn't resent that she was expected to study hard and make good grades, and she did. She loved her parents and it was obvious that she was the center of their world. If they had reservations about him, they didn't show it. As long as he followed their rules, he was allowed to spend time with her.

As his hopes were raised they also fell and fluctuated up and down like a roller coaster. It was like trying to keep a stage act going that had nothing to do with his real life. As much as he tried, he couldn't quite believe that he was good enough for Kristy and he worried that the true reality of his life would be exposed before he could have her for his own. He questioned what would happen after she was faced with the truth. He thought of every possibility. If he had enough money, he could take her away. Maybe she could be convinced to run away with him, elope as his parents had done, build a new life somewhere else, and then she'd never have to know. But that wouldn't work either because she loved her parents and would not want to leave them. She had nothing to run from and would be miserable living away from a place where she was genuinely happy. He found it ironic that because she was happy, she had a generous spirit that kept her from seeing the badness in him or sensing that he was capable of acts of vile wrong-doing. These were the thoughts and fears that plagued him during the spring and summer and fall of that year.

Then a harsh winter fell upon the mountains. Ice storms littered the roads with splintered trees and broken branches and road crews worked from dusk to dawn, clearing and cutting, their chain saws buzzing and chippers grinding and flatbeds hauling the piles of lumber away. Schools were closed for days at a time and power outages kept linemen working into the night. Travel on mountain roads was limited to absolute necessity. Bobby was put to work at home keeping the firewood piled high and the property maintained while his father was held up on the coast working there. Bobby's friends were in the same boat and Kristy was sheltered in her protected environment, helping her mother and studying by firelight. March brought with it a record-breaking snowfall and April followed with high winds blowing in from the coast accompanied by a hailstorm that dented metal roofing and dislodged still-hanging broken tree limbs, pummeling them with a barrage of miniature ice balls until they fell, requiring another month of road clean-up and structure repair.

When spring finally took hold and mountains burst into bloom, spring fever affected everyone, but none more than the youth who had been so unbearably confined. When the school doors opened and released them to an early summer, fragrant spring blossoms mixed with summer blooms and the air was permeated with the pungent scent of mimosa and sweet honeysuckle.

On a bright moonlit night on a trail that led down to the riverbank, Bobby led Kristy by the hand and she followed with full knowledge of his intentions. Their passion had reached a heated intensity that was palpable. She'd been fearful and indecisive. He'd anticipated her anxiety by bringing a mason jar of elderberry moonshine that looked like a fruit drink. He offered her a sip to help her relax. She drank it obediently, gasping for breath and then calming from its tingling effect. She drank it once more and the warmth spread through her body like sunshine, her translucent skin enhanced by the moon light. Bobby thought he had never seen anyone so radiant and told her how beautiful she looked. And she felt that way the whole time it took him to undo the buttons down the front her flower-print summer blouse and help her unzip and pull down her jeans. And then, in the sweet hours before midnight, on a pine needle bed by the river, with silver moon rays streaming down, lighting up her skin to the color of pearls, they were lost in excruciating bliss and total abandon.

Another hour passed before he took her home. It was past her curfew and the porch light was shining too bright, like a warning beacon. Shame had descended somewhere along the way and he saw it in her eyes. After going inside, she didn't reappear at her upstairs window to wave goodnight to him as she usually did. And after that night, no matter how many times she smiled and reassured him after their intimate encounters, he always knew that the shame was there and that he was the cause of it. They had the rest of the summer ahead of them and another year of school before graduation. Her parents had her future planned while his lay before him like a void. He'd not been groomed for college, the war in Vietnam was over, his father had never discussed his future, and his mother seemed not to care.

The military was still an option, but his school record would pose a problem, and he'd need permission from his parents if he tried to enlist before he was 18. He'd been made to feel learning disabled and perhaps that was why there'd been no higher learning expectations. But it seemed more likely that his father had his own plans for him, plans that would keep him dependent. There was always money to be made helping him with his ventures and unscrupulous schemes, but that income could end at his father's whim if he ever gave the slightest hint of opposition or betrayal. Without a choice, he'd become his father's apprentice and a necessary part of his functioning. He'd been discouraged from having other aspirations, been beaten down psychologically under his father's control, tainted and corrupted in the process. And now he had made Kristy part of it.

While Bobby continued to build a case against himself in his mind, his relationship with Kristy deteriorated. Insecurity about his future did not dispel his desire for her, but he drank more alcohol to relieve his insecurity. He started showing up for their dates inebriated and began sabotaging their relationship with erratic behavior that upset her. She forgave him for the first few incidents and then started making excuses not to see him. He suspected that she had confided in her parents and that they were behind it; Kristy would do such a thing, be honest with them about her concerns and he knew they would be alarmed and protective. He responded with anger and defiance, revealing to them the side of him he had initially tried to hide.

Kristy broke up with him. Bobby convinced himself that he had ruined things between them for her sake. But he couldn't shake off his need for her. Losing the one person he longed to be with propelled his anger into rage, which he medicated with alcohol and a further descent into depravity, accompanied by his trusty band of marauders. There were hunting raids and senseless acts of violence unleashed by firelight on moonless nights beneath starless skies when blackness covered the sprawling timberland and coyotes howled in unison. There were other girls and other drugs with which to experiment. His sex drive expanded to include the antithesis of what he'd been naturally attracted to, an almost rebellion against it: the wild young girls from disreputable city dweller families and rowdy hard-drinking mountain clans, fast and loose, no rules and no limits, attracted to the bad boys of the forest and their leader.

By autumn of that year after school was back in session and his father was back on the home-front, he eventually came back to an unsettled center, regained control of his mood-altering substance intake, and lessened his time with his gang. He realized that he'd had a self-defeating reaction to the loss of his first love, and he vowed to not let it happen again. He had his last year of high school to finish and his father to contend with, who once again had plans for another trip to the coast. But this time, Bobby had a plan of his own.

His father might have picked up on the changes in him had he not been especially busy that year. Job and business demands had been keeping him more occupied than usual and sporadically away from home. They'd been hunting and poaching together less frequently as a result, but their annual trip to the coast was nearing. Bobby had turned 16 that year and had come to terms with authority by exerting it over his gang. By following his father's orders he'd learned to give orders, and he'd continue to take them until he no longer had to. In the meantime, he was stuck in a two-way chain of command with his gang at the bottom and his father at the top. He'd come to this conclusion while learning about and developing leadership abilities in the subterranean existence he'd created in secret while still living under his father's rule. He even wished he could tell his father about it and show him that he wasn't making stupid mistakes anymore, that he, too, could have power over friends, overcome the loss of a girl, have sex when he wanted to, drink his fill and deny himself and let him know that he'd become a man. But he knew better. He'd have to impress him in some other way, and soon.

An opportunity presented itself, as he thought it would, during their trip to the North Carolina coast. Their yearly father and son outing had become a ritualistic journey in which Bobby was continually put to the test, he knew that now, had come to expect it. Once again, Robert had located a seemingly bountiful hunting area on private land owned by a man he'd met during a seed marketing inspection. He'd already checked out the man's property and surroundings and chose a point of entry that was a safe distance from the main house and a likely spot for deer. It was accessed down a stretch of private road posted with a "No Trespassing" sign. The property was fenced but had damaged places where climbing over it wouldn't be difficult. Near one of them, he'd carved a notch into one of the hickory tree fencing posts.

Using night vision gear to see, aided by the light of a moon on the rise, they encroached upon the man's land early one morning before the sun came up. They'd had a problem finding a place to hide the car due to a recent trimming of brush and timber by the designated area. The car was left only partially hidden and not far enough off-road, which was careless. This worried Bobby from the onset but that was not unusual. He'd always been amazed at his father's contemptuous disregard for signs and postings and notifications of private ownership. These warnings to him were like a red flag to a bull. He hunted where he wanted to hunt regardless of the consequences, and took each warning as a dare and a challenge, and if caught, another reason to do harm to someone.

It had taken Bobby a long time to understand the full extent of his father's actions from beginning to end. He had once believed that poaching the game, the kill, the catch, the bounty, was the ultimate goal, but had learned that the goal was the game itself, a game of chance, win or lose. And his father was a very, very bad loser.

The plan was to get in and out before dawn and be on their way back to the motel. But they stayed in too long trying to spotlight game that must have caught their scent and fled. Dawn was breaking, and as luck would have it, the landowner was an early riser and liked to drive around his property at daybreak to check the perimeter for fencing repairs. When he spotted the car, which he might have missed had he just been driving by, he wrote down the muddied-over license plate number and drove back to his house to call the county sheriff. In the meantime, they had made it back to the car and back to the motel without realizing that their vehicle had been spotted.

The next day, a warrant had been issued and they were picked up. Bobby was told to remain silent while his father gave a valid argument for the car being parked in such a way off a private road in a posted "No Trespassing" area. But he did not want to call attention to his identity, should the landowner appear in court and recognize him, so he paid the fine instead of fighting the charge in court, which he probably could have won. After all, he surmised, there was no real evidence to support the claim by the owner that they'd been poaching, they had left no evidence behind to be discovered, and there'd been no game found in the freezer chest in the trunk of the car. Beyond that, although their car was parked on the man's property, it could not be proven that they had driven it there or driven it away.

The hefty fine was a bitter pill for his father to swallow, despite the fact that they were guilty. He felt he'd been tricked by the landowner, reason enough for a vendetta to start taking shape in his mind. Beyond that, his concern that the man might recognize his name and possibly report him to the Department of Agriculture for taking advantage of knowledge obtained while on the job was added cause for a retaliatory plan of action.

There was no conversation about it. The next few days passed without incident as they fished the coastal waters and went about their normal vacation routine. But Bobby was like a barometer for his father's moods and felt his rage build day by day, knowing what it meant, wondering how it would be expressed, watching for a sign, for the opportunity he'd been waiting for.

It didn't come until they were on their way back to Asheville and well out of Hyde County. They'd been traveling for about two hours and it was almost dark. There was something about the dusk that evening that heightened the senses. Darkening shadows, milky gray clouds, and transparent violet-blue mist blended together in a ghostly dance of movement that swirled over the highway and stirred the anxiety and tension between them into a wicked brew of intent that percolated until it reached its peak. The car veered off the interstate onto an exit ramp and came to a halt.

His father said, "We're going to get him for this, Bobby. He's going to pay."

Bobby would vividly remember that moment, that hour, and the thrill of anticipation as they sped back down the highway toward the coast. He'd felt amped up, intensely alive, glancing periodically at the set of his father's jaw, knowing that the time had come to show him what he was made of. The time passed by as quickly as the mile markers and exit signs until they came to the one directing them to the road and the man who had made the mistake of accusing them of poaching.

The exit sign triggered a rush of excitement and a memory

that flashed into his brain like a headlight, one from a lost time in his boyhood when he'd still been in his father's favor. He recalled a night when they had been sitting around a campfire and his father had been railing on about the misuse of the word "poaching." He said it was an old English word, meaning "The Kings Game," and told about how he'd been brought up to believe he had the making of a king, was as good as any of them, and would not think otherwise, and would take his rights where he saw fit and woe to any man who stood in his way. And then he said,

"The same blood that's pumping through my veins is pumping through yours, boy. And don't you forget it."

The yellow moon was big and round and rising and his father cut the lights using only his night vision to see. He turned at the entrance to the man's driveway and drove slowly to a spot under a canopy of trees where he had a view of the lighted house and from there scanned the well-maintained yard for something to destroy. He'd watched his father devise a plan of destruction countless times while waiting for instructions, for orders. But this time, on impulse, taking the moment in hand and this one chance to impress him, he reached for his 22 rifle, put on the silencer, and said to his father,

"I'll take care of him."

Robert stared at him intently for almost a minute, and then replied,

"Don't kill him, just cripple him."

Equipped with his two-way radio and scoped rifle, he reached the house and the lighted windows and tried to see inside. Two of them were curtained but when he moved around the corner and came upon the third window, he could see a man sitting in a chair watching T.V. He backed away, keeping the man in his view until he could only see the side of his head and part of his upper body. He crouched behind an ornamental tree in the yard and rested the gun on one of its branches and then lined the man up in his crosshairs. He pulled the trigger.

It was just that quick. The man slumped over and he waited for another few seconds followed by nothing but silence and then walked back to the car and got in. He felt exhilarated, like he'd passed some imaginary rite of passage. He'd demonstrated his power, his manhood, had shown his mettle, taken control of the situation, and completed it with efficiency and accuracy. Mission accomplished; the dividing line between life and death blurred.

He could not recall when it happened, when the conscience that had once kept him awake at nights had been finally locked away in a vault so secure that it could no longer escape to haunt his dreams. He had lived through an emotional war that he had won, or so he believed. He rationalized that if he had gone to war, a real war, he'd have been a good soldier, an asset to his commander, fearless and brave; the enemy would have been chosen for him, just as his father had done. The enemy was simply a target, the reason not to be questioned. If he started to question any of his actions, he might as well put a bullet into his brain.

Instead of questioning, he waited for a sign of approval from his father. But once again, he got an unexpected reaction. At first Robert just stared at him quizzically, his piercing blue eyes studying him like he was looking through a microscope. And then his expression began to change and his lips curved into that sly grin, that deadly awful half-smile of self-satisfaction that held not one iota of praise, and he said in a half-joking way,

"You'd better remember this, Bobby. Now I've got something on you."

Bobby's mind reeled. So all it had meant to his father was that they were finally even? Since that day on the flatboat when he'd challenged his father, he'd been ridden and berated, punished and ignored, treated with mistrust and constantly pressured, and it had all come down to this? He had to shoot a man to balance things out? Nothing he'd done before this had made a difference, even when he'd thought it had, even when he'd tried to do everything he could to make up for it. None of it had meant anything. Up until he'd pulled that trigger, he'd been seen as an enemy, a threat, someone who might talk, who might betray him, who was no longer a son.

Oh yes, he would remember this night. It was the night that covered his heart in blackness and chained him to the Machiavellian authority that was his father. Incredibly, he'd finally gained some importance, some usefulness as his father's partner in crime. He'd evened out the balance by becoming a dangerous felon who could be turned over to the police if he got out of line.

His small band of followers waiting for him back in Asheville seemed like children to him now. But they would continue to serve him well by supplying him with alcohol he would have to rely on to remain impervious to feelings that might try to invade his steel-encrusted soul.

CHAPTER ELEVEN

I felt their eyes. I knew what they wanted, and so I turned to
look again upon the almost empty clothes, the flash of bone so pale and
curving. But I would give them nothing, and my body did not betray
me, for which I was grateful. For what I felt was the return of a long-
quiescent rage, and the certain conviction that this was the most human
my father had ever appeared to me.
— John Hart, The King of Lies

Bobby worked as his father's henchman until he was almost
18, while continuing to develop his own enterprises and associa-
tions in secret. And then things started to change. His original
gang had disbanded after several of them had dropped out of
school. Those who remained close to him until after graduation,
like Johnny McCabe, helped him recruit replacements to join
them in poaching forays into the forest. He began to seek out
real hunters, people like him, and became more determined to
have a life independent from his father, not realizing how much
like him he'd become.

His only escape from the crimes he continued to commit for
him was found in the wilderness. In a sense, it was a psychological escape into a place that his father made claim to but could
not control. Being a woodsman had been his true calling since he

was a small boy. He considered it the one good thing he'd done on his own, before his father began teaching him, before he was forced into submission and a life of crime. He'd barely been out of diapers when he had fearlessly run outside into the woods and been chased and caught by his grandmother before he had gone too far. Left in her care for weeks at a time, she allowed him to venture a little at a time until giving him the freedom to explore on his own. And when he returned to her, after hearing her call to him, he'd bring something of the wild to place in her hands. And always she would praise him and encourage his love of the natural world.

It was the only world he knew in which he had a chance of salvation, although salvation was as far from his mind as redemption. But there was something at his core that yearned for an indefinable future and a way of life akin to nature. In the forest the rules were not governed by man, but by nature itself, and the killing that was done made some sense. Killing wasn't done for revenge, for some minor slight, for some underhanded scheme, for cheating someone out of a few dollars. It was done for food and survival. Hatred had nothing to do with it; animals didn't kill because they hated, they killed to eat. They didn't kill for revenge, even if one of them ripped its prey into bloody shreds and devoured the heart; it had nothing to do with revenge.

The rest of his life was a mindless blur during that time. He drank and used drugs, began collecting an assortment of weapons, became increasingly violent, and the jaded partnership with his father deteriorated into a test of wills, a competition. Things between them went from bad to worse when Robert found out about some of his activities and ranted like a jealous rival about his loser friends and associates. Bobby fought back by staying away from him, coming home late at night or not at all, threatening to leave home for good.

Then something started happening that tempered Bobby to some degree. There was a change in his father that made him appear more vulnerable, an increased paranoia, frequent descents into brooding black moods that would last for days at a time and endless talk about government agents and spies. His obsessive thinking was exacerbated when Julius warned Robert that he'd brought suspicion on himself for exacting revenge on too many people. Even his cronies in Asheville were beginning to keep their distance. Some had risen to higher plains of social respectability and elected political office, one was even considering running for congress. None of them wanted any form of scandal. The climate had changed and the volatile 1960s were over, the social revolution tamed, and his father had become a liability. Bobby was beginning to see him in a different light.

His mother was eligible for retirement after twenty years at the courthouse and was encouraged by her boss to take it, as her health was beginning to decline. Life had not been easy for her. She rarely saw her parents, and her father was in poor health. Bobby visited his grandparents once in a while but felt awkward in their presence, like an alien from the dark side of the moon. He dealt with his father by spending less time at home and more time carving out new territories and opportunities. He wanted independence and income, and realized he had to get a handle on himself to make this happen. In an odd way, he seemed to be gaining strength from his father's weakened condition. The tables were turning and some of his old discipline was beginning to kick in.

He began by moving in different circles through contacts made at guns clubs and local bars that drew in the type of people he sought out, bootleggers dealing in alcohol, drugs, and firearms. He had no qualms about dealing in illegal trade but also understood the hierarchy involved in these organizations and started hanging out in places where the right connections could be made. This was a step out into an arena where he was not a leader but a young intruder, but one with the wiles and nerve to do it. He'd been taught by the most intimidating man he'd ever known and understood the power of violence in gaining respect, and the wisdom of giving respect to those who were in power. He analyzed every situation he found himself in and began to adopt a persona that fit in to these environments. He armed himself accordingly and assumed a new street name, Bo. Before long, he gained acceptance, partly because he had something to offer from his own illegal dealings and crew of followers, but most importantly, he'd won over the people who ran things because he gave them their due and followed orders without question.

For the first time in his life, he had money to spend and a bad reputation that worked for him instead of against him. When he walked into the hangouts he frequented, he was treated in a friendly manner by the older men he admired who got a kick out of his audacity, and this had a restraining effect on the younger ones who still had something to prove. When he went to the gun clubs, his manner was different. He talked to other hunters and weapons collectors and learned from them like an eager student, watching them buy and sell and upgrade their collections, while adding to his own personal arsenal. He met men he admired there, men who reminded him a little of CB, weekend hunters and sportsmen, respectable men who were not in "the life." And they responded to his need for their friendship. He was even encouraged to join the Freemasons.

But when he went home, his father tried to treat him the same way he always had, like a bumbling idiot, trying to break his confidence down by chinking away at his ego, just as he had done with his mother. And she was fading away right before his eyes, home all of the time now, subject to continual criticism and nothing left of herself to give.

Instead of rebelling against his father, Bobby now looked at him with contempt, staring straight back at him when confronted, looking into the deep dark blue pools that used to terrify him and seeing them glaze over with craziness. Even his cruel words had little weight and meaning to him now, and had lost their power to defeat him. Instead, he'd walk out, staying away for days at a time, but always coming back home. He needed to show his father at every juncture that he was coming into his own, that he could no longer be controlled. He had to be there to witness the decline of the man who had ruled his life, ruined his youth, infested his spirit with hatred, and who depended on him more than he had realized. He wasn't ready to make the break, not yet, maybe never; there was too much between them, as painful and contentious as it continued to be.

Once he was "established" in Asheville, he'd thought he'd made it, having reached a comfortable plateau and finding a niche for himself. His ambition was limited to his local surroundings until one night when he made some new acquaintances. He was standing at the bar in one of his favorite hangouts, Annabelle's Restaurant and Lounge. The beer was cold and he was enjoying the atmosphere, partly because he had a little 7-Up bottle filled with white liquor hidden in his jacket pocket. Every so often he'd take it out and add a shot to liven up the beer he was drinking. Unbeknownst to him, the hawk-like, street-wise eyes of a mobster named Nick Scarpetti were observing him from a corner table in the restaurant, 7-Up bottle and all.

The next thing Bobby knew, a man who stood approximately 5 feet, 5 inches tall, weighed about 400 pounds, and looked like a well-dressed bull, tapped him on the shoulder and said very politely but firmly,

"Excuse me, sir." Then he looked toward the corner table.

"Mr. Scarpetti over there would like for you to come and sit and have a drink with him."

Bobby looked across the room at the men sitting at the table. All were well-dressed, with slick jet black hair and darker skin than he was used to seeing in Asheville.

Trying to project a bold attitude, he accepted the invitation by saying,

"Of course."

He followed the fat man across the room and sat down in the extra chair that was brought to the table for him by the waiter.

The fat man introduced the man sitting directly across from him as "Mr. Scarpetti."

Scarpetti nodded to him and asked, "What are you drinking, kid?"

Bobby replied, "Beer would be nice."

"What's that in your coat pocket?"

"Which one?"

Scarpetti gestured toward his right pocket.

Bobby replied, "A .38 snub-nose," and then pulled it out far enough for the man to see the handle and cylinder.

Scarpetti's companions lurched back in their chairs and one said, "Holy shit!"

Scarpetti exclaimed, "Jesus Christ, kid, who you gonna kill?"

Bobby replied, "You never know."

Scarpetti continued, "What's in the other one?"

"A small bottle of white liquor."

"Can I try a shot?"

"Oh yeah," Bobby said and then passed the bottle to him.

Scarpetti drank a sip and then passed it around to the other men at the table and each one took a drink. They appeared to like it a lot. They continued drinking and talking together for a while and then Scarpetti asked him to walk out into the parking lot with them to settle a deal in private. Bobby agreed to go back over the mountain to the still owned by one of his recent suppliers. Scarpetti wanted him to bring back two cases of moonshine for them to take back to "Philly," where they were from.

Bobby learned that Nicky Scarpetti was the crime boss of Philadelphia. Scarpetti learned that Bobby could regularly supply him with moonshine and fresh venison. Over a period of time he became Scarpetti's regular supplier of liquor, wild game, and silencers for their guns. Later on, once he'd gained Scarpetti's trust, he was kept "on standby" for other work, like "taking out the garbage down there," which meant disposing of someone in the vicinity, or taking care of whatever dirty work needed to be done. His work for Scarpetti would eventually give him the credentials he needed to be accepted by other members of the mafia. But this was his first experience in the criminal big leagues and he was only beginning to earn them.

CHAPTER TWELVE

No matter how big a guy might be, Nicky would take him on.
You beat Nicky with fists, he comes back with a bat. You beat him with a
knife, he comes back with a gun. And you beat him with a gun, you better
kill him, because he'll keep comin' back and back until one of you is dead.
— *Ace Rothstein (Robert De Niro)*, Casino

The nicknames started to accumulate by his early twenties; Bobby was known as Bo-Guns, Bo-Blades, Bo-Diesel, all representing his exploits. His life was cranked into high gear. He'd formed partnerships with moonshine and weapons suppliers, and his team of poachers continued to invade the Biltmore grounds and the Pisgah forest. The game wardens were on to him and traps were set up everywhere. There had been many close calls and one shoot-out during a car chase from Biltmore Village to the Mills River area in which their get-away vehicle was riddled with bullets. They had escaped capture that night and spent the rest of it in a body shop owned by an associate working until dawn removing every sign of damage and hiding away every carcass of evidence.

There were regular runs to Philadelphia and a supply line was established between his growing crew in Asheville and Scarpetti's syndicate. Philadelphia was a major hub for drug distribution in the United States and Scarpetti's connections in North Carolina were primarily mob related; Bobby worked outside of that network as a separate entity. He was a phenomenon of sorts because it was unusual to be trusted by any mob boss in that way. When problems arose within Scarpetti's organization or his connections in Asheville, Bobby would take care of them like a mercenary coming out of the fog and retreating back into it again, leaving those connected wondering how it had happened and who within the local syndicate was responsible.

At night, he was leading a life of decadence. During the day, he was aspiring to something he'd never been part of before and knew little about, the Freemasons. It was a path he wanted to follow and thus put forth an effort to make a good impression on his friends who were collectors and sportsmen, and then take one of them up on his offer to sponsor his petition to join. He remembered that his father had once tried to join the Freemasons and been denied membership. His reputation, more infamous than Bobby's, was one factor. Another was his high level associations; some of the members knew him personally and had grave misgivings about his acceptance. Robert was thought of as a lone wolf, a little too dangerous for their liking, too unpredictable, and he made some of them feel uncomfortable.

Bobby was much better at developing his relationships; there was a quality about him that was appealing to those who befriended him. He was loyal to a fault and far less selfish than his father. He gave back much in return, too much, possibly out of gratitude and more probably out of his need for approval. Robert on the other hand had never needed approval, except for a brief time before his father abandoned the family. He'd been raised since birth with praise and attention lavished upon him and it had made him self-centered and demanding, incapable of lavishing it on anyone else. Once Robert had weaned Bobby away from his mother and her parents, he'd deprived his son of praise, doling it out in little bits and pieces like a miser; his miserliness borne of selfishness.

Robert drove Bobby to search elsewhere for the approval he so desperately needed and he found it working in a criminal environment for a man of power who had put his trust in him and awarded him with some level of recognition. That Bobby was attending to his needs in an underworld made up of thieves and cutthroats had not been apparent to him, nor had he been aware that the best qualities he had brought forth to gain acceptance had been twisted into monstrous deviations.

Coinciding with his service to Nick Scarpetti, he was also seeking acceptance into another environment, one more uplifting and with a group of men he aspired to emulate. He'd been running on a mixture of alcohol and adrenaline and knew that he needed to slow down. It was not the first time he had tried to find his way out of the darkness. He had tried to with Kristy, but had not been able to overcome the powerlessness of his situation back then. This time, however, he hoped that he could, and felt empowered by his decision to join the Freemasons.

After his petition for membership had been submitted, he had to swear that he was a man of legal age, good reputation, and possessed a belief in God. Although it was true that he was of legal age, and did believe in God, he'd been living a godless life and the only place he had a good reputation was with the small group of sportsmen who'd encouraged him to join. He was grateful that, despite many close calls, he'd not been arrested since reaching adult status and had no criminal record that would have prevented his membership. It was then left up to the members of the local lodge to decide his acceptance. When they did, he'd been greatly relieved and felt honored. Having been treated like an outcast for most of his youth, the idea of belonging to a secret organization that called itself a brotherhood was something he treasured immensely and in this he was distinctly different from his father; he wasn't doing it to use anyone.

His father was still in the picture like an old soldier trying to hold onto a command he had lost and a campaign he was no longer part of. And yet they gravitated toward one another as father and son, father not willing to let go and son throwing into his face what he had become. Bobby let his father know that he'd been accepted into the Freemasons and knew that he'd hit a sore spot that would fester like an infected wound. If the Freemasons had been made up of one man, his father would have planned to destroy the man. But he would not go up against an entire organization, so he tried to make Bobby feel like a fool for joining them. It didn't work, nothing was working with Bobby anymore, and it frustrated the hell out of him.

Bobby's membership in the Freemasons came at an opportune time because it had a stabilizing effect on him and he felt included. His work for Scarpetti was on the outside of a mob organization that was closed to him. He'd been good enough to supply their needs and take care of their "dirty laundry" but he would never be accepted into the Italian mafia. For one thing, he wasn't Italian and had no chance of ever being a "made man." The mafia had its own secret rites and rituals and hierarchy and he could have no part in them. The exclusion bothered him more than he had let on, even to himself. He had not felt part of anything substantial until joining the Freemasons; it gave him a sense of belonging.

As he began to learn more about freemasonry, he became fascinated with the subject and the nature of this secret society. He quickly became a history buff when he learned that two of his heroes, Davey Crockett and Sam Bowie, had been freemasons. He was amazed at the worldwide scope of the organization and that it dated back to the Middle Ages. He learned about its origins, how some believed freemasonry was an outgrowth of medieval guilds of stonemasons, directly descendent of the Temple of Solomon in Jerusalem (the Knights Templar), and offshoot of the ancient Mystery schools, an administrative arm of the Priory of Sion, the Roman Collegia, the Comacine masters, intellectual descendents of Noah, and other various origins. Others argued that freemasonry began much later in the 17th century, having no connection to earlier organizations.

The precise origins didn't matter as much to him as the freemasons' history of providing a haven for revolutionary nonconformists and their sympathizers during times when rebellion of any kind could result in one's death, which was the reason for their tradition of secret meetings and handshakes. He learned that according to Masonic legend, the stonemasons constructed a lodge building adjacent to their work site where they could meet. When the early lodges began including members who were not actual stonemasons, they started meeting in taverns and other convenient public meeting places, and employed a "Tyler" to guard the door from intruders, informers, and the curious. Instead of meeting in the work-site stonemason lodges, the group itself became the "Lodge" wherever they met and became a lasting tradition.

And in North America, Masonic Lodges known as "Blue Lodges" founded a collection of Masonic groups with names such as York Rite, Scottish Rite, and The Shrine, but the dues were still paid to the Blue Lodge. The Blue Lodge and its ceremonies established the fundamental bond which made all freemasons "brothers" and bound them all together. There were also lodges formed by groupings of persons with similar interests or background, such as "old boy" lodges associated with certain schools, universities, military units, or businesses, even small cities and counties, accepting members from almost any religion, like-mindedness being the criteria.

Bobby was accustomed to the "old boy" network that ran Asheville because of his father's involvement in it, but the "old boy" group within his freemason lodge was even more politically connected than he'd imagined. He recognized some of the older men as friends of his father, but they had no recollection of him. These men accepted him for how he behaved when he was with them and didn't seem to associate him with his father or question him about the activities that provided his income. He'd been successful so far at living a dual existence; he was also beginning to develop a duality of thought provoked by what he was reading and learning about freemasonry.

He was most interested in their broad interpretation of belief in God which included a naturalistic view of God, different from the Bible teachings he'd learned from his grandmother. It was like learning a new spiritual language that represented a multitude of beliefs that were melded into one central theme. In the end, he decided to stick with his grandmother's "good Lord" thinking; he didn't need any other gods to look down on him with disfavor.

In his lodge, membership was limited to men only, who promised to uphold the principles of "Brotherly Love, Relief and Truth." The moral lessons he learned were taught through rituals, by degrees. He found some of the moral lessons confusing, like being expected to become involved in public service and charity work in order to demonstrate the value of his membership. This was a foreign concept to Bobby. He'd been raised to believe that charity begins at home and when he lived at home, charity meant his father.

Unlike his father, he'd always been generous with his friends when he could be, especially after a lucrative deal had gone down, but he hadn't really done anything to help anyone else. He did know a biker club that raised money for crippled kids so he didn't think it would be embarrassing to do something like that, but spreading money around was something that might bring attention to him that he didn't want. He had to give that moral lesson more thought.

Besides, he was supposed to be in a secret society. The freemasons had been the ones who practically invented the idea and showed others how to do it. He was fascinated with their system of secret modes of recognition, like the secret grip designed to allow members to recognize each other even in the dark which had started the whole business of secret handshakes. They'd invented hand gestures that were covert signs and special identifying passwords based on Hebrew words that were taken from the Old Testament and many other secret codes. They had modes of recognition that varied over time to indicate different jurisdictions and lodges.

But what he found most amazing was their reliance on architectural symbolism. The medieval stone masons were the ones responsible for this; they ingeniously used their tools of the trade to form the principal symbols, like the square and compasses arranged to form a quadrilateral—the square used to represent matter, and the compass to represent the spirit or mind. The square was also said to represent the world of concrete or the measure of objective reality, while the compass represented abstract or subjective judgment.

Bobby didn't understand it completely but wasn't intimidated by the concept. He had grown up learning mountain codes and their symbols and signs and mouth to ear communications, a language so intricate that his father's innate knowledge of it led him to be chosen as a cryptographer and developer of secret communications for the Navy during the war. He was proud of his father's achievements despite the bad feelings he felt for him, and grateful that he'd been taught by such a master.

As he delved more deeply into the history of the stonemasons he began to feel kinship for these early rebels who understood that even though they worked in stone, nothing should be written in it that would make them vulnerable to discovery. So their symbols were taught by word of mouth to be recognized at sight with all their full meaning. A symbol of the compasses straddling the square represented to them the interdependence between the two, and in the space between the two there was sometimes placed a blazing star or symbol of light representing Truth or Knowledge, or sometimes a letter G to represent God or Geometry. The Supreme Being or God was sometimes referred to as the Grand Geometer or the great Architect of the Universe. Because much of the symbolism was mathematical in nature and in particular geometrical, freemasonry later attracted people of more rational beliefs such as George Washington and Benjamin Franklin and Mark Twain.

Bobby felt elevated by this knowledge and being part of an organization that had attracted such men. Although he continued to believe in the God of his grandmother's teachings, he was beginning to feel some hope that God might understand that he had been oppressed too, like the early masons had been. He was no longer confined to one way of thinking or believing and this was giving him room to grow in his mind. He thrived within the freemason rituals and consistencies while feeling freedom in their acceptance of people's differences. The square and the compasses were displayed at all Masonic meetings, along with the open Volume of their Sacred Law, upon which the oaths were taken. He learned that in most English speaking countries the Holy Bible was used as the Volume of Sacred Law, but it could also be any inspirational book of scripture or even a blank book in lodges where members had many different beliefs.

He was at the initial degree of the freemasons, an "Entered Apprentice." He wanted to ascend to the "Fellow Craft" degree, and then to the third degree of "Master Mason." As he studied his lessons and began to interpret them for himself, he began to question his life and discuss topics with some of the older men. They told him stories about the difficult paths of other freemasons, some of whom were famous, like Mozart who used Masonic symbolism in his opera, *The Magic Flute,* and the British author, Rudyard Kipling who used the Masonic myth and symbolism in his stories. He had heard of these men but had never thought of a composer or a writer as being rebels. But as he learned more, he began to see how free-thinking men could be viewed in such a way. Freemasonry had started as a subversive group, but it was formed to fight tyranny. It had become one of the oldest organizations in society, respected for its good works but still viewed as subversive and was often misjudged, targeted by conspiracy theorists, or seen as an occult or evil power associated with a New World order bent on world domination. The world power theory arose from the fact that so many political figures in the past 300 years had been freemasons. What he did notice within the organization was the practice of cronyism and exchanging favors, and one member giving another an increased chance for employment.

Bobby felt somewhat defensive about the negative impressions of outsiders, comparing his experience within the freemasons to his experience within the criminal underworld, and wondered if any of these accusers would like to see where the real evil power existed. As for Satanic rituals, the only ones he'd heard of around the mountain areas took place in certain parts of the forest where small groups of Satanic believers, mostly young screwed-up delinquents, gathered to drink blood and plan grave-robbing and desecration raids on local fundamentalist churches, and they had nothing to do with the freemasons.

Bobby figured that most of the misunderstanding probably stemmed from the Masonic initiation ritual he had taken in which he had sworn an obligation or "blood oath" wishing severe punishment upon himself should he ever reveal the secrets of freemasonry to a non-Mason. He understood this as a tradition that was viewed as a psychologically powerful way to express a serious bond or promise. He'd been told that in some jurisdictions, there had been an effort to appease criticism by changing the oath to "bloodless oaths." But his lodge adhered to the traditional ritual and explained to him that the bloody punishments mentioned in the obligations were references to the punishments that the state at one time inflicted on the defenders of liberty and religious freedoms, such as freemasons.

They told him about conspiracy theorists who went so far as to look at certain historical murders and deduce that they were done as a fulfillment of a blood oath. Some even said that Jack the Ripper was rumored to have been a freemason who was made psychotic by carrying out a blood oath and killed his victims in the same fashion. Bobby's mentors assured him that the mutilations had no similarity to the symbolic punishments of the obligation oath and reminded him that the only 3 penalties he could impose as a freemason was censure, suspension of membership, and expulsion. Bobby wasn't worried. He could give them examples of expulsion in the criminal world that would make Jack the Ripper look like an amateur.

He was more impressed that so many presidents, such as James Monroe, Andrew Jackson, James Polk, James Buchanan, Andrew Johnson, James Garfield, William McKinley, Theodore Roosevelt, William Taft, Warren Harding, Franklin D. Roosevelt, Harry Truman, Lyndon Johnson, and Gerald Ford were freemasons, as well as other famous Americans such as John Hancock, Paul Revere, and another hero of his, Sam Houston. He was astounded to learn that Abraham Lincoln had petitioned to be a member while running for U.S. Senate and had been denied, just like his father, but was later inducted after his death by the very lodge that he had petitioned to join.

Bobby's interest in these facts and his ability to remember them was revising his opinion of his learning capabilities. If he, in truth, had a learning disability, how could he have done this? It made him angry to think that he had so easily bought into the label they had given him at school. He'd acquired much knowledge in a very short period of time because first, he'd been interested in the subject, and second, because he'd been treated as though he *could* learn it and was someone worth educating. His freemason mentors had done something for him that no teacher had done. He'd always had a tendency to self-analyze, but this time his analysis was positive and inspired him to exercise his brain in the same disciplined way he had exercised his body. And this was a revelation to him, marking another turning point, but one that would unfortunately be delayed for some time because he was about to run into detours that would take him back into the darkness again, blind him from the light, and block his progress toward salvation.

There were many warning signs before he made the first

detour. They came in the form of symptoms that started with lower back pain and red-colored patches on his skin. At first he thought he was having an allergic reaction to something, remembering the symptoms that CB had described and he'd witnessed. But his were different. He tired easily, felt achy all over, and developed a low-grade fever. His skin was itchy, which drove him nearly crazy, and then he started having night sweats. He cut back on alcohol but the symptoms continued. When he started losing weight, he finally went to a doctor.

After being put through a battery of tests, Bobby was referred to an internal medicine cancer specialist, Dr. Michael Messino. Dr. Messino practiced in Asheville near the Mission Memorial Hospital, which was located less than a mile from the Biltmore Village. He was a no-nonsense physician approaching age 60, who had a non-judgmental approach to his patients. Raised in an Italian neighborhood in New York, Messino was a devout Catholic who attributed his success to God's divine hands. His deep faith had inspired in him a desire to help others, to be a healer, and had driven him to work his way from the rough neighborhood where he was born into the prestigious halls of higher learning by working as a welder. After an internship at Johns Hopkins University School of Medicine, he came to North Carolina's Duke University School of Medicine for his residency and decided to stay, setting up practice in Asheville. He'd been around long enough to know the people of his area and he wasn't easily shocked. But his first impression of Bobby was immediate and alarming. He could read the life of a person by looking into his or her eyes and what he saw in Bobby's struck him as tragic. What he observed in his physical appearance was a toughened and tattooed young man with a body as hard as a rock, weakened by a condition that he could almost diagnose without examination or testing. During the physical, Dr. Messino discovered that the nodes of Bobby's neck and shoulders felt rubbery and were swollen. Bobby winced with pain when Messino touched them. A chest radiograph showed the lymph nodes of his chest were also affected.

Bobby told Dr. Messino that he'd been having pain after drinking alcohol, sometimes within minutes after taking a drink. He described the pain as sometimes sharp and stabbing or dull and aching. Messino had him admitted into Mission Memorial and ordered an excisional biopsy, blood tests, and a Positron emission tomography (PET) scanning. When the test results came in, Dr. Phillips' initial suspicions were confirmed and Bobby was diagnosed with Stage IV Hodgkin's disease.

When Dr. Messino gave him the news, Bobby's new hope of a forgiving God reverted to the belief that God's wrath had finally descended upon him. He listened in shock as Messino described Hodgkin's disease as a cancer originating from white blood cells called lymphocytes and abnormalities in the lymph system. He explained that the lymphoma is typically characterized by the orderly spread of the disease from one lymph node group to another and by the development of systematic symptoms as the disease advances. He said the Hodgkin's lymphoma could be treated with radiation therapy, chemotherapy or hematopoietic stem cell transplantation. He indicated that the choice of treatment depended on the age group he was in, his male sex, and the fact that he was at Stage IV of the lymphoma.

Bobby had difficulty comprehending what he was hearing, his defenses too weakened to fend off the words that were hitting him like blows from a fist. Messino kept on talking about Hodgkin's disease typically occurring in two main age groups, young adults 15 to 35 years old and adults over 55 years old. In the younger group, there was a 10-year overall survival rate for cases of early diagnosis. Bobby worried that he had waited too long before being tested, but Dr. Messino encouraged him to believe in his recovery and gave him the continual support and individual attention he needed to fight his negative prognosis. Messino put it to him in a way that hit home by telling him that perhaps God might be giving him a warning rather than a final execution.

So the chemotherapy treatments began and he approached the study of his disease in the same way he had the study of freemasonry and found there were no guidelines for preventing Hodgkin's lymphoma because the cause was unknown. Risk factors were varied and included being of the male sex, being in the young adult age group, a family history, having had mononucleosis or Epstein-Barr virus, a weakened immune system, HIV or AIDS, use of human growth hormone, and/or exposure to exotoxins such as agent orange. Although he had minimal knowledge of his family's medical history, he came to the conclusion that his immune system had been weakened by his lifestyle.

During his stay in the hospital and afterward, when he returned home to stay with his parents during months of outpatient treatment, the tension between Bobby and his father lessened, but little sympathy was afforded. Robert treated him as though he had brought the disease on himself. Bobby was too sick to fight with him about it and stuck to his regime of medication and chemotherapy with plodding, step by step perseverance.

He was told by the hospital staff of physicians and nurses that he was responding to treatment remarkably well and his prognosis became more hopeful with each stage of his regimen. But Bobby attributed his road to recovery to Dr. Messino, who treated him with unusual warmth and compassion. He wondered at this Italian man named Michael and came to believe he had saved his life. It would not be the last time an Italian by that angelic name gave him a chance for redemption. But that came later.

His life otherwise had stopped on all fronts as he traveled from home to hospital and from hospital to home, avoiding contacts and disappearing from the scene, like a monk in retreat. But his mind was in a total state of action as he reevaluated his future on a daily basis. Stuck at home in the midst of the dysfunction he'd been raised in, he listened to the same old diatribes, the constant bickering of his parents, his mother now arguing back as his father was becoming more dependent on her and more impossible. The memories flooded in, the medication allowing them to, and he could not find a spiritual path to lead him away from them, even when it was sparked in him that he should, simply out of gratitude for his recovery. He was instead diverted once again away from the light and this time the trail wound its way toward a faraway murky distance where a new frontier of danger, intrigue, and depravity awaited.

CHAPTER THIRTEEN

> *Sadly, sadly, the sun rose; it rose upon no sadder sight than the*
> *man of good abilities, and good emotions, incapable of their directed*
> *exercise, incapable of his own help and his own happiness, sensible in the*
> *blight on him, and resigning himself to let it eat him away.*
> — *Charles Dickens*, A Tale of Two Cities

He had to get out of there, out of his father's house and out of Asheville, and he wanted to get as far away as possible. Against the odds, he was on his way to full recovery and had renewed strength and vigor, but was jaded again by his surroundings. His time spent at home in recovery had been a nightmare of emotional regression, so much so that he wanted to break away, go anywhere, get as far from his father as he could. But he needed money and he needed connections and instead of returning to the freemasons, he returned to the nightlife scene to make his presence known again. Although thinner and a bit gaunt, he projected the appearance of robust health and gave no indication of the struggles he'd been through during the previous year. He didn't have the luxury anymore of seeking spiritual enlightenment. He had to be on the move and separate himself from the man who'd been driving him to drink again. It was in this state of mind that he was making the rounds of clubs one night and ran into an old friend from his past.

Roger Thompson was an "ol' boy" he knew from one of the rowdiest mountain families around. They were a rough bunch and had always been and had ties to his father dating back to his bootlegging days. Bobby liked Roger and knew that he was trustworthy. After they talked for a while, Bobby described his predicament and Roger's face lit up with excitement. He told Bobby about a friend of his, Ricky Bryson, whose father owned a local trucking company, said he'd talked to Ricky recently, who told him that his father was looking to hire a bodyguard. He explained that Big Jim Bryson spent most of his time on the road working as a long-distance truck driver and that his company was a front for a syndicate operation he headed called the Dixie Mafia. Bobby let him know that he was interested and Roger recommended him, through Ricky, for the job.

Bryson dealt mainly in methamphetamines (crank or crystal meth) and cocaine, importing his products to and from Los Angeles and Asheville. Bryson had been a long-time distributor of illegal liquor and other goods until getting involved in the drug trade. He'd always had a larger view of things due to his cross-country travels and built up his customer base on his truck routes throughout the country. He was a man who liked sizable profits and recognized early on the money that could be made in trafficking meth supplies. He was savvy and ruthless, and had connections in every city and small town he traveled through and knew each place as though he'd lived there for years. Bryson was born with an internal map that enabled him to see the big picture and create a trade route structure for his business that kept him on the move.

But things had changed dramatically in Mexico since the drug lords from other regions of South America had started moving in and taking over, creating an influx of new operations in the Southwestern states and in and around Los Angeles. Bryson's competition was growing, and so were his list of enemies from deals gone bad and his methods of retribution for non-payment. He'd had several incidents of ambush and attempted murder and needed someone with him who could give him protection on the road and during his stopovers and also help him with his trade. Bryson checked around and found out that Bobby's name still carried some weight in Asheville and hired him on the spot. Bobby assured him that he was the man for the job.

Bobby went with Bryson everywhere, especially when they were delivering a supply of dope to the Outlaw Bikers Club. The Outlaws were a very dangerous group of fellows who were known to kill at the drop of a hat. But Bobby impressed Bryson right off the bat when he handled their first attempts to intimidate him by making it known that he carried a .45 in one pocket and a hand grenade in the other, and had no reservations about using either one. Bobby had been educated in the use of explosives by his father. He'd adapted this knowledge to create a personal arsenal that made him a greater threat to those with whom he came in contact. He'd had some reservations about his ability to deal with gangs in territories that were new to him. He had no affiliations there other than Bryson and had to have an edge. It made Bryson nervous, but it also made his adversaries back off. Bobby had adopted a theatrical Rambo approach to recreating himself, and it paid off.

Bryson also had connections with a head of the Mexican Mafia in Los Angeles named Pancho. Pancho would send loads of meth to Bryson's other phony trucking company in L.A. called J&B Trucking, whereupon they would weigh the merchandise and package it according to need. Bobby would then be sent with money to Western Union and send it to a name supplied by Pancho. Business ran smoothly for a while until Big Jim put a wrench in their spokes.

It wasn't the first time Bobby had seen this trait in him. Bryson's stubbornness and other idiosyncratic behaviors continually reminded him of his father. They were about the same age and were both penny-pinching and mean and would spend a dollar to save a dime and kill someone over a nickel. And there was no reasoning with either one of them. At times he couldn't believe that he was working for a man who was so much like the one he'd left Asheville to get away from. And this was just another incident to prove it.

A big load of cocaine had come in from Pancho and the quality was down. Bryson, who looked for any opportunity to reduce the agreed upon amount of payment, refused to pay the full price, so Pancho refused to ship any more until he did, maintaining that the quality was the same. The bikers were waiting for their delivery and everything was on hold. Bobby had been dealing with the bikers and tried to convince Big Jim to take the bad with the good, a practice he had learned in the poaching trade where there were always variations in game quality, fur and hide. Moreover, Bobby knew that dealers like Pancho, who were closer to his age group, were not going to take Bryson's behavior lightly. He'd disrupted a movable feast of drugs and the customers were waiting and growing impatient. And Pancho, who operated in the immediate, was not going to be slowed down by an aging tyrant who was still operating the way it had been done in the old days. Bobby understood this clearly but he also understood the nature of the beast he was dealing with.

Just like his father, when Big Jim thought he was right, he would dig in his heels and demand his own way until he got it. He didn't listen to Bobby's counsel and was even planning a retaliation scheme in case Pancho didn't concede to his demands. Bobby's respect for him was slipping fast and brought to his mind a memory of something his father had made him do when he was in his early teens.

The episode involved a Ford Tractor & Supply in Asheville. His father had taken a faulty tractor part he had to the tractor supply to exchange it for another one. The parts salesman did not recognize the part as their merchandise and refused to make the exchange. It was an ongoing effort of his father's to score an acquisition without cost; he was an opportunist who would cheat on any deal if he could get away with it. And when things didn't go his way in the bargain, the other party would pay in one way or another. In this situation, he left in a fury because he hadn't been able to pull the wool over the salesman's eyes. He'd been with his father at the tractor supply and when they got home, he'd ominously said,

"Come on, Bobby."

He'd followed his father downstairs into the basement where he got a gallon-sized container into which he poured one half-gallon of sugar. When they returned to the tractor lot, his father filled the rest with diesel fuel. They sat there waiting until no one was around and then his father handed the container over to him, pointed to the most expensive tractor on the lot, and told him to go over to it and pour the contents into the fuel tank. This would cause the tractor's engine to seize up when running and destroy the engine. The tractor was a 17,000 dollar machine, its engine ruined for a simple part that cost no more than 12 dollars. For this they took a chance of being caught, being arrested, being incarcerated, and being sued.

He found it ironic that he now found himself in the company of a man who was capable of the same type of unwise risky retaliations, but playing with higher stakes and deadlier consequences. Bryson was no match for members of the Mexican Mafia, although he thought he was. When he'd organized his Dixie Mafia, he'd patterned it on other illegal syndicates; but the more Bobby learned about Bryson's organization, the more he realized that it was no more than an informal old boy network spread out across the country made up of groups he had formed over which he tried to maintain authority. And it had worked for him as long as he kept the product coming and going and benefiting those with whom he did business. The internal structure of his organization was not nearly as sophisticated as the Italian mafia. Bobby was educating himself in the intricacies of these organizations and was beginning to see similarities between the Mexican and Italian organizations, and even the Freemasons, in terms of structure and hierarchy. Bryson was playing out of his league and Bobby was feeling increasingly uncomfortable working for him.

In his dealings with the bikers and Pancho, he'd learned enough about the Mexican Mafia to fear them, fearless as he tried to be. Their organization, started in 1958, was formed from one of the oldest and most powerful prison gangs in the United States. They were involved in extortion, drug trafficking, and murder, both inside and outside the prison system. He'd gained knowledge of their ritualistic practices while running errands for Bryson and had been fairly successful because he was practiced in the art of survival, knew what to look for and what to avoid.

He was, after all, a tracker at heart. His knowledge of mountain codes and freemasonry symbolism also helped and it didn't take him long to grasp the significance of their signs and symbols, the primary one being the image of a black hand. The "black hand" was often used in their tattoos, representing the national symbol of Mexico (eagle and a snake) atop a flaming circle over crossed knives. Street gangs aligned with the Mexican Mafia (known as La Eme, the letter "M" in Spanish) often used the number 13 as a gang identifier, as the letter "M" is the 13th letter of the modern Latin-derived alphabet.

Bobby's experiences with Nicky Scarpetti and the free-masons prompted him to find out more about Pancho's world because he understood the advantage of using this knowledge when doing business with him and his associates. In the early 1960s at San Quentin Prison, two felons, Luis Flores and Rudy "Cheyenne" Cadena, established a blood oath for members of the Mexican Mafia. The oath stipulated that the only way for a member to leave the organization was to be killed. Flores and Cadena also established a set of gang commandments such as: a new member must be sponsored by an existing member; there had to be approval from existing members to join; the gang had priority over family; existence of the Mexican Mafia had to be denied to law enforcement or non-members; respect had to be paid to other members; street conflicts which existed before in-carceration had to be forgiven; and execution of a member of the gang for rule violation had to be committed by the gang member who sponsored him.

The Mexican Mafia was known for its unmerciful acts of violence and brutality, machete mutilations and other savage methods of inflicting terror on enemies. They were also the con-trolling organization for almost every Chicano gang in South-ern California and their membership extended to other states including Texas, Arizona, and New Mexico. Members of almost all Chicano gangs in Southern California were obligated under the threat of death to carry out any and all orders from "made" Mexican Mafia members. And this was the force that Bryson was ready to challenge by getting into a dispute with one of their heads.

Bobby pleaded with Bryson to use some sense. Bryson re-fused to listen to his advice and became angry because Bobby wasn't supporting his position. In a fit of anger, he went to L.A. on his own to "straighten Pancho and those wetbacks out" and left Bobby behind to take care of the business and the local bikers, who had stopped complaining and started threatening.

After a week went by with no news from Bryson, Bobby knew what had happened. He continued to open the J&B Trucking business to maintain appearances and answer the phone. One day it rang and Pancho was on the line. He exchanged pleasantries with him as if nothing had happened. Bobby went along with it for a few minutes and then asked, "Where is Big Jim, Pancho?"

Pancho replied, "He's gone."

"What do you mean?" Bobby asked. "Is he on his way back to Asheville?"

"He's gone and there's nothing you can do about it."

"Oh, that's where you're wrong, Pal. You don't know me. There's plenty I could do about it. But I ain't emotionally involved. I'm here for the money."

"I heard that about you. I think I will trust you. I like the way you think. Me and you, we gonna start this business back up and you gonna take Big Jim's spot."

Bryson owed the Mexicans $100,000. Bobby was the only one who could open the safe, which held a total of $55,000 in cash. He told Pancho the truth. Pancho instructed Bobby to send $50,000 of it, distribute the drugs that Bryson had withheld from the bikers, and he would send 12 pounds, 5 kilos, more or less, of meth to get the purchase and delivery flow going again. They measured in pounds because that was the way they shipped it. He told Bobby he could pay the remainder of Bryson's debt with what he made from selling and distributing the new shipment, and if he was smart, he'd have enough left over to purchase the next load and be back in business. Pancho was, in a sense, fronting him, but he was doing it for his own purposes.

Bobby felt no remorse about Bryson. He'd been with his father time and time again when his greed and obstinacy had overridden his judgment and gotten him or them into trouble. The audacity that had made his father a legend when he was young, when he had driven the thunder roads of Buncombe County like a swift marauder, daring the revenuers to catch him, when he'd plundered the estate grounds and forest for game, testing the game wardens to their limits, when he'd crafted secret codes and decoded those sent by the enemy during the war, impressing his commander, when he'd cruised the streets of Asheville with his war hero reputation, winning the heart of his mountain princess, the reckless courage that he'd possessed then had over the years turned into the same vengeful stupidity he'd seen in Bryson. When Big Jim took it upon himself to go off without him to "straighten out Pancho," Bobby had ceased being his bodyguard. Bryson had gotten what he deserved, and that was that.

With Bryson's disappearance, Bobby had moved up from bodyguard to boss of his own small syndicate. Over the next year, he set up a base of operations in Asheville, using Bryson's J & B Trucking and Tire Company front. Bobby had informed Bryson's immediate family of his death and some of the circumstances surrounding it. They weren't surprised that he had come to a bad end and made no claim to ownership of the phony trucking company. Bryson's son, Ricky, who was a drug dealer with no head for business, went to work for Bobby. There was some initial tension and distrust between them, but Bobby kept him in line and the relationship was profitable. They used Fed Ex shipping and UPS to move drugs back and forth between Pancho's organization in L.A. and Asheville. The drugs were hidden in one of five tires in every stack and transported across state lines to be delivered to rented storage buildings.

Bobby also maintained a good business relationship with Pancho, communicating with him regularly while putting together his own small crime family made up of trusted contacts in Buncombe County. He reconnected with Nick Scarpetti's organization and re-established a drug, liquor and weapons pipeline from Asheville to Philadelphia which he triangulated to include Bryson's old trade routes to and from L.A. Then he set up a new business front to replace J&B Trucking. He named it Blue Ridge Excavating Company and structured his business to be run from the top down. He attended to every detail of its formation.

Through the excavating company, he purchased and supplied parts for bulldozers. He devised a method of hiding drugs within steel pipes. Once the drugs were inserted, the pipe would be packed with cotton balls and welded together and then wrapped and sprayed with deer scent, which drug sniffing dogs were trained to ignore. A covering was then placed over the pipe and welded; the result appeared to be an apparatus on a bulldozer arm. The subterfuge was successful from the onset and his shipments met all of their destinations without a hitch. Business grew slow and steady and consumed all of his time. He lined up one shipment after the next, overseeing every aspect of the operation, tracking each delivery, wiring money to get the next shipment paid for, always needing at least $25,000 up front for each L.A. order of $50,000 worth of merchandise. The best customers for delivery were in Scarpetti's organization because the mob had the money to pay up front, so this link kept the product moving and the money coming in as long as he was consistently reliable. The demand was never a problem. Meeting it required his full attention.

The process of building a loyal team took more time. He got rid of people from Bryson's organization whom he didn't trust and surrounded himself with a selected few whom he did, just as he had with his first gang in high school. He'd also learned from Bryson's mistakes and developed a knack for resolving problems and managing his subordinates. He came to realize that he had some of his father's charismatic attributes and began to access more fully this aspect of his personality, developing a persona that was both winning and intimidating.

His enemies were primarily his competition and he tried to make alliances to fend off takeover attempts. He'd been wise to keep his organization small and tight-knit, naming it "Robert's Raiders" after *Rogers Rangers* of pre-revolutionary war fame. He had a flare for the dramatic, having been raised in a territory where a reputation could become a legend, and he found this appealing. It added a colorful dimension to his status and reframed in his mind his criminal enterprise into a rebel cause. But his rationalization was skewed, there was no "just cause" to fight and no honorable "rebel yell" to cry. The only war going on in the country was the one being declared on drugs and the traffickers who distributed them. And unlike his father, he did not go to war in defense of his country. He went to war against it.

The illegal drug market in the United States at that time was one of the most profitable in the world. As such, it attracted the most ruthless, sophisticated, and aggressive drug traffickers in the business. Drug law enforcement agencies had upgraded their efforts to protect the country's borders; about 116 million vehicles crossed the land borders with Canada and Mexico and more than 90,000 merchant and passenger ships docked at U.S. ports, carrying more than 9 million shipping containers and 400 million tons of cargo. Another 157,000 smaller vessels visited the coastal towns. Amid this voluminous trade, drug traffickers concealed cocaine, heroin, marijuana, and methamphetamine shipments for distribution in U.S. neighborhoods.

During the 1970s, more diverse criminal groups began trafficking illegal drugs. Groups operating from South America smuggled cocaine and heroin into the United States using a variety of routes, including land routes through Mexico, maritime routes along Mexico's east and west coasts, sea routes through the Caribbean, and international air corridors. Groups operating from neighboring Mexico smuggled in cocaine, heroin, methamphetamine, amphetamine, and marijuana. In addition to distributing cocaine and methamphetamine in the West and Midwest, these Mexico-based groups were now attempting to expand the distribution of those drugs into eastern U.S. markets. Demand for methamphetamine was increasing, especially in the West and Midwest, and with it the number of illicit laboratories working to supply the growing number of meth addicts. The use of cocaine and crack cocaine was spreading from urban environments to smaller cities and suburban areas of the country, and violence and criminal activity was growing rampant.

The U.S/Mexico border was the primary point of entry for cocaine shipments. Cocaine was then distributed to nearly all major cities in the United States. Organized crime groups operating in Colombia controlled the worldwide supply of cocaine. These organizations used a sophisticated infrastructure to move cocaine by land, sea, and air. In the United States, they operated cocaine distribution and drug money laundering networks comprising a vast infrastructure of multiple cells functioning in many major metropolitan areas. Each cell performed a specific function within the organization: transportation, local distribution, or money movement. Mexican drug trafficking organizations were used to distribute multi-kilogram quantities of cocaine and were becoming increasingly responsible for the transportation, and it was the link with Pancho's cell of operation and the takeover of Big Jim Bryson's that started Bobby on his way down the road to perdition.

Where Bryson had been able to envision the wide scope of his syndicate operations as a collection of cities and towns, each with a collection of people inside them, Bobby envisioned his territory as a vast primeval forest where danger lurked at every turn, unseen, faceless, and ready to strike. He'd seen savagery done in the human wild-life kingdom of Los Angeles that made the Asheville and the French Broad region seem like a haven of security. But the French Broad River that ran through his veins had a history of violence deeply embedded in the genetic memories of those raised along its banks. If the coursing waters that had washed over the bones of scalped and mutilated corpses after Cherokee and settler raids and retaliations could speak, they would tell tales that would give the Mexican mob a few lessons in cruel and unusual punishment.

One historian wrote that although there were no large battles or major engagements fought on the scale of those outside the area during the Civil War, there was no region in the state which endured more violence over a comparable period of time than the mountains of North Carolina, that acre for acre there was probably more gratuitous cold-blooded murder during that time than there was in any four-year period of the Wild West. Cut off and unmonitored, a great deal of fratricidal raiding and bushwhacking occurred between small bands of men under no regular military command. A New York Tribune reporter, who had escaped prison and stayed there with a group of Union sympathizers, wrote: "During our whole journey we entered only one house inhabited by white Unionists, which had never been plundered by the Home Guard or Rebel guerillas. Almost every loyal family had given to the Cause some of its nearest and dearest. We were told so frequently—'My father was killed in those woods' or, 'The guerillas shot my brother in that ravine,' that, these tragedies made little impression on us."

No matter which side was chosen, the battles fought in this singular mountain theater of war created divisions between neighbors and kinfolk that were more personal than those fought on large faraway battlefields and stories of brother against brother, neighbor against neighbor atrocities ran through family bloodlines for generations. Nothing was forgotten, or forgiven. The mountain people kept these stories alive through their oral traditions and their collective memories were embedded in the psyche of their offspring. These influences later played out in long-standing feuds and clannish political allegiances that would erupt into vicious unscrupulous campaigns and elections. Crime became a natural offshoot of politics just as criminal behavior was viewed as a natural form of rebellion against any imposed system of law.

And all of this bloody drama played out before a scenic masterpiece, a backdrop of undulating and alluring beauty that belied man's darkest intentions and most dastardly actions. The murdered bodies that had over time been cleansed in the mountains' rivers, and decayed back to nature beneath the soil of its forests, were crimes no less vicious than those garishly displayed in scenes from other places and cities or found baked and abandoned under western desert skies, they were just more camouflaged in a magnificent cloak of lush greenery that made the bloodshed seem less stark and glaringly wrong.

If Bobby had had any degree of reservation or conscience about his actions before he took over Bryson's operation, he lost it setting up his own. He was now part of the ebb and flow of the drug trade business, energized, ambitious, and ready to roll.

The government's crack-down on drug dealing and distribution did not dissuade Bobby in the least. He was not just fighting a war with the government he was fighting a war within himself. He was in a state of rebellion against authority and running wild through a forest of his imaginings, convincing himself that he was no different from the rebels who had revolted against the government during the Whiskey Rebellion, those who had settled into the mountains and survived against the odds. His rationalizations were fueled with alcohol, adrenaline, and a feeling of power that was growing with his success, the most intoxicating drug he had ever experienced.

He'd become "The Man" in Asheville, the main supplier of meth supplies in Western North Carolina. He was playing in the big leagues and could pick up a phone if he had a problem with someone and have "the garbage taken out." Killing was nothing in the arena in which he operated. It was the cost of doing business and in this business, the consequences were severe.

Bodies were wrapped in chains and disposed of in deep water lakes, cemented into concrete blocks, dissolved in acid baths in places like an auto shop near Asheville where bumpers were re-chromed, or cut up like a deer torso and buried in shallow graves or under hollow logs or dug-up tree trunks, with 50 pounds of lime added to speed up decomposition. It was the way things were done in the despicable underworld in which he lived.

It was a tough business and Asheville was a tough place to be in business. For the very reasons that he had rebel leanings, the same inclinations applied to many others at the underbelly of Asheville. Unlike Philadelphia and Los Angeles, criminal opera-tions in Asheville were not dominated by a terrifying mafia fam-ily, but by an inter-linked network of operations independent from one another and yet bound by common threads of illegal enterprise. The people involved were not afraid of organized crime as an overpowering unit and therefore could alter associa-tions and loyalties to suit their own purposes. They would not be ruled by any unified omnipresent organization, whether state or federal government, or mob-related. The mountain codes that thrived for centuries against changing laws and authorities were invented by the people from mouth to ear, clan to clan, settle-ment to settlement within a wilderness more fearsome than any man, or any group. The very nature of this phenomenon had made it possible for a young lone wolf like Bobby to congregate a small mob and build a powerful niche for Robert's Raiders within a territory teeming with crime and corruption.

In order to maintain power and security, Bobby relied on in-formation gathered by his informants at local clubs and hang-outs. He decided it would be to his advantage to be part owner in one of them, so he invested a portion of his profits to buy 12% interest in the Lone Dove Saloon, one of the most popular bars in town. He took the position of "head of security" as a cover and began to become a more visible presence at the saloon. His reputation had preceded him and he worked at creating an im-age that fit with local expectations, enjoying the attention and respect he received when he came into the room. He was "the man to see" and a method of distribution was set up at the sa-loon to supply customers with his products. Drugs could be or-dered at the bar if the customer knew how to order them from the bartenders. Certain drinks, like a *Singapore Sling*, represented an 8-ball (an industry term used to describe an 8th of an ounce of heroin mixed with crack cocaine), at $250, a *Blue Motorcycle* represented an ounce of cocaine.

When the word got out about his meth supply, business picked up substantially. And so did the risk, because it meant that he was warehousing drugs in Asheville instead of shipping them out immediately after receiving. He was also no longer limiting distribution locally to a chosen few. By widening his local circle of trade in Asheville to a greater extent than ever before, he was headed down a dangerous path, but could not see it. He was young and full of muscle and drive, impervious to warnings by his underlings, and beginning to believe his own hype. The attention he was receiving was going to his head, but another more seductive factor impaired his judgment completely.

He was falling in love, and it was the kind of love that fed his ego and made him feel invincible. She was not just a typical drug-dealer's girl; they were everywhere and sex was always available. A man with dope and money to burn could have his pick of the women who frequented the clubs looking for a good time. The women who were attracted to men in his business were a breed of their own, drawn to the dark side of life and the tough guys who wielded power within it. And they found in these men a vital source of protection and reflected glory, a beneficial position in an otherwise tricky walk-on-the-wild-side lifestyle. Some were passed around like candy, and some were taken like poison, using their bodies to obtain drugs and liquor or fulfill other needs. These women were often abused and degraded. Others held their own with the men, but few were an intricate part of the business. Most were there for the party, the ride, and held on for dear life in the midst of it. And then there were those who stood out, and one who rose above them like a queen of the night.

The first time he saw her, Bobby envisioned a wild dark horse with a black trailing mane running ahead of the herd, free and graceful, denying possession, entrapment, or being broken into submission. Her name was Shelley and she was beautiful, gorgeous, and barely out of her teens. She came into the bar one night on her own seeking independence, looking for excitement, and stopping him dead in his tracks. He made claim to her before anyone else could approach her. After he did, no one dared. She was "the Man's girl" and she was with him all the way, falling hard for him and the money and the good times. A decade younger, she looked up to him but also had the over-confidence of youth, not letting him get his own way, demanding more than he'd ever given, and expecting his total devotion. And he let her have her way, shared with her his spoils and spent more on her than he'd ever spent on himself. She was smart and fun to be with and loved to travel by his side.

It wasn't long before Shelley was making her own trips to different locales and banks. She'd learned how to make cash drops for him, setting up savings accounts with cash deposits of under $10,000 in each designated bank in order to obtain lockboxes at each location. After establishing an account, the much larger amounts of money would be placed in the safety-deposit boxes. For each transaction, he'd give her $5,000 to blow, a 5-G present she became accustomed to, along with other perks he gave her. But Shelley also proved to be trustworthy and efficient and he grew to depend upon her completely. She was not just a dope-dealer's girl; he believed that she could have been anything she set her mind to be, and it affected him deeply that she chose to be with him. But it also made him more reckless and intensified his need to 'up the ante' in order to increase his cash flow, and this led to allowing more people into his business, and he did so with less caution, relying on his reputation rather than his valuable time to keep people in check. Over time, Shelley took the place of his closest associates and one of them was becoming less trustworthy and more self-serving. A seed of betrayal was being sown in the ground below him while he was riding high in the sky in a cloud of self-delusion.

CHAPTER FOURTEEN

It is the same for all men. None of us can escape the shadow of
the father. To be worthy of that man, to prove something to that man, to
exorcise the memory of that man from every corner of our life—however
it affects us, the shadow of that man cannot be denied.
— Kent Nerburn, The Wolf at Twilight

Information about his operation was leaking out. A crooked cop in Asheville named Bart Edwards started showing up to shake him down. It was a warning sign that something was off-kilter. The false sense of security he'd mistakenly fostered began to evaporate. Paranoia set in like a bad cold he couldn't shake. The old bad memories intruded his thoughts on a daily basis, leaving him shaken and temperamental, reminding him of his boyhood attempt to gain confidence and some semblance of control only to have it swept away in one fell swoop by the massive hands of a merciless tyrant.

His consumption of alcohol increased and so did his need for reassurance from Shelley. But she couldn't understand the change in him. He hired a bodyguard named Blaine and didn't go anywhere without him. It was on his mind that all of his methodical planning and countless innovations during the building of his organization, all of his efforts and achievements in his rise to power, even his emboldened persona and empowered sense of self, could be destroyed just as swiftly as his father had done that day on the flatboat, and he'd never see it coming.

He thought of his father almost daily now, the man who would never recognize what he'd accomplished but who had contributed greatly to his success. After all, he was the one who taught him to steel his heart against compassion, molded him into a mercenary, taught him the pecuniary art of business, exemplified the knack of manipulating others and garnering fearful obedience rather than true loyalty, and showed him how to put himself first above everyone else, paying heed to no greater power than himself. In one respect, however, his father had failed. He had not crushed in Bobby the ability to love.

Bobby had rediscovered this ability when he fell in love with Shelley. He thought he had lost it when he lost Kristy. He even realized that his love for Shelley might be his undoing, but he couldn't stop it and didn't want to. If his life was to be a fast and furious rise and fall, then "so be it," because he'd managed to do something and find something that years ago would have seemed impossible.

The days and then months passed without incident, but the strain on his nerves continued. Unfamiliar faces appeared in the Lone Dove and the atmosphere grew tense whenever he was there. There was too much money on hand and too many drugs. Shipments that he kept in continuous process were now only part of his priorities. Local supply and demand had increased significantly. Meth supplies and other drugs and weapons were warehoused in rented storage bins and too often stored within the secreted vault in his private residence, a rustic cabin he'd purchased on a parcel of woodland located on the outskirts of the city. He had other safe-houses scattered around in locations unknown to even those he trusted, and had brought his parents into the scheme of things after taking the advice of a customer by the name of Ralph Morgan.

Ralph Morgan was a heavy-hitting CPA for a large supermarket chain. He also had a cocaine problem and was afraid to buy it from anyone but Bobby, whom he'd come to depend on. He operated in the legitimate world of business and lived in

Asheville, but was drawn to its dangerous playgrounds where blackmail, robbery, and murder were not uncommon. In addition, Morgan liked to have parties, big parties, where the liquor was plentiful and the cocaine was served on platters with canapés. He was a good customer, would buy 4 ounces of cocaine at a time for just one occasion or for his own recreational use. His coke parties were legendary within certain circles and gave him access to the party girls and side of life that made his otherwise mundane existence bearable. He admired Bobby in many ways, his swagger and style, his audacious approach to life, and his well-armed ability to elicit respect. He relied on Bobby to protect and supply him, and Bobby did.

One night, after they'd sat talking in the late hours before closing time at the saloon, Morgan asked, "What are you doing with all the money you're making, Bo? You work hard for it and take a lot of risk. Are you sure you have it protected? If you were to be caught, and the probability is that eventually you will be, they could take everything you have away, what you've got stored in the banks, and what you've got hidden. They can find it, too, after they tear your life apart looking for it."

Bobby listened to his sober warning and it gave him pause. He'd been having premonitions, feeling that things were closing in on him.

He replied, "What do you suggest?"

Morgan advised, "Invest a large portion of your money in your mother's name and then she can give it back to you as an inheritance."

He then proceeded to outline the details for Bobby and helped him to make the necessary arrangements. Bobby retrieved $100,000 from his back-up vault that was built into the basement floor of his home by a construction company carpenter ally who'd installed his safe. His mother was agreeable to the plan and his father put up little resistance. They no longer had control of him and his mother had been fading away for years out of sheer helplessness and hopelessness. But it was still unlike them to be so cooperative, particularly his father. The money transfer and his parents' willingness to go along with it had been too easy. Bobby wondered if they, too, might have been having premonitions about his future, and the thought filled him with dread.

Back at the Lone Dove Saloon, he continued to maintain a high-profile as head of security to cover his business interests, and although his guard was up, his habits had become routine. He usually arrived late, when the place was packed, the country-rock music blaring on full-tilt boogie, and the denim and leather clad crowd were united in drug and alcohol induced camaraderie. Sometimes there would be a momentary pause when he came through the door. If Shelley was with him, heads turned toward her. Shelley was a show-stopper, but he was a threat. The combination of the two of them seemed to shift the air in the room sideways, and when it centered back, the party continued. However, there were eyes of interest that remained focused on him, shifty and subdued, never apparent. They watched as he checked in with his subordinates, the bartenders who were under their supervision, and his co-owner who gave him an update on the evening's take before leaving for the night.

Bobby closed the bar twice a week and was the last one to leave when he did. He'd have Blaine take Shelley home around midnight and return to wait for him outside as a security measure while he went over a final calculation of the drug sale profits and prepared the cash for deposit. The rest of the cash would be locked in the office safe and his cut stuffed into a money-bag. In the meantime, Blaine was expected to do a security check of the parking area before bringing the four-wheel drive, tinted windowed, extended cab cobalt-black Chevy Blazer around to the back door exit from the private parking space allotted for it, and wait for him there. Bobby would lock up, hop into the rear custom-designed section of the Blazer and shove the money-bag into a hidden compartment where it would remain secured until the next morning when Blaine would drive Shelley to the bank where the money would be placed in a safety-deposit box.

But one night, Bobby's routine was interrupted by three half-rate thugs, two of them brothers, who had for weeks been setting up a plan to rob him. Blaine was viciously attacked from behind when he got out of the Blazer to check out the parking lot. His head was split open with a claw-hammer and he was left unconscious and bleeding, kicked over against the base of the extra-wide back tire of Bobby's vehicle. When Bobby came out of the saloon, the cash bag strapped beneath his shoulder next to the gun and holster inside of his jacket vest, he'd set the door to lock behind him before he realized that Blaine was not there waiting for him. He knew immediately that he'd made a mistake and his senses accelerated to high alert.

Just as suddenly, out of the darkness, a man approached him with a purpose that was evident, despite his attempt to appear otherwise. Bobby's quick assessment took in everything: the strange glint in the man's eyes, his shaky hands, poorly tied boots, awkward gait, tense expression, the nervous twitch at the corner of his mouth. He had appeared to be unarmed and non-threatening in an attempt to get closer, to put him off guard. But Bobby knew that he was carrying and could see the bulge of the weapon under his light jacket and wondered why he hadn't pulled it out.

The man asked, "Do you have change for a $100 bill?"

Although most of it was covered by the man's hand, Bobby recognized a portion of the bill as a 20, not a 100 dollar bill. In response to the man's bizarre appeal, Bobby reached into his vest pocket as if to withdraw money and drew out his pistol instead and pointed it at him. A minivan screeched around the corner from the parking lot. Immediately, Bobby understood. He'd apparently come out of the back door before they were ready for him and the man in front of him had been trying to stall him until the others arrived, too scared to take Bobby on himself. The passenger side door of the van opened before it came to a stop and a big burly guy wielding a shotgun got out. The driver was gunning the engine and remained inside the van. The man in front of him moved back a step, reaching for the weapon he should have had out in the first place. Bobby shot him in the chest, right beneath the clavicle. When he slumped over, Bobby hit him in the head with his pistol and then raised it toward the man coming toward him with the shotgun.

Bobby had gained the advantage in a matter of seconds. He ordered the man with the shotgun to drop his weapon. Realizing that their plan had gone terribly wrong, the heavily built bearded man threw the shotgun to the pavement. The driver of the van kept revving up the engine as if in a panic. The man he had shot groaned in pain and the big man looked down at him, stricken at the sight. Blood was spurting out from the wound, turning the front of his jacket red; his body was quivering and right leg jerking. Smoke was coming out of his back from the bullet hole as air was expended. The big man looked up again at Bobby and pleaded, "God, man, he's my brother, just let me take him out of here. Please man, we made a mistake, just let us go and you'll never see us again."

The man at his feet moaned loudly as if knowing his brother could hear. Bobby didn't need this mess. The shot was probably heard and reported to the police. The last thing he wanted was attention from the law. He ordered the burly man to get his brother out of there and held the gun on him until he'd half-drug, half-carried his much smaller sibling to the van, shouting to the driver to speed away. The van jolted forward before the door closed and they raced away, screeching tires and breaking every traffic law in their path.

Bobby stood there momentarily shaking his head, knowing that his quick response and reflexes had saved him. If they'd had the slightest edge, they would have shot him dead as soon as they had the drug money. They'd been stupid and slow and yet, had almost succeeded. But he'd been even more careless, too predictable, too distracted by other things. His mind raced and then he said to himself in disgust, "What the hell is happening? First that rogue asshole Edwards thinks he can mess with me and take me for regular pay-offs, and then these slow-witted cretins thought they could rob me. What a goddamned fiasco."

Bobby's jaw tightened as he refocused and went to search for Blaine. He found him lying by the Blazer, returning to consciousness, the nasty gash in his blood-soaked head needing medical attention. He'd been felled before having a chance to defend himself. It would be a devastating blow to his ego, but he'd survive. The days were numbered, however, for the men who were responsible for his injury.

It was a bad omen. And it started a chain reaction. Bobby wasted no time gathering information about the brothers. Their last name was Whalen, from a miserable clan of moonshiners that lived over near Candler; the driver was a dupe they ran with from Haywood County. They weren't well known except for petty bootlegging crimes and misdemeanors. He suspected that they hadn't been working alone, had been put up to the robbery by someone with inside information. There was a Judas in his midst whom he had to identify, and he'd felt it for some time.

The Whalen brothers had taken responsibility for the shooting, blaming it on a family quarrel. Claimed they'd thrown the weapon in the river so the police wouldn't try to trace it back to him. It was their way of trying to make amends, to buy back their lives. But the cops didn't buy it. The gunshot had been treated by a doctor and reported, coinciding too closely with the gunshot reported near the Lone Dove Saloon. Blood traces had been found by the saloon's back door and they were making other connections.

After the shooting, the word was out on the street. It was as if people knew before and after what had gone down in the parking lot that night. The bloodhound nose of the law was close to the ground and sniffing everywhere, and everywhere they were picking up his scent. They had already come to the conclusion that the only thing that would have prompted the Whalens to go after someone as dangerous as they believed Bobby to be, from what they were being informed, was a major stash of drugs or drug money.

Their informer was a man named Keith Branch, who had been an on-the-fringe contact when Bobby first bought interest in the Lone Dove Saloon. He'd gained Bobby's trust while helping him to organize the bartenders and train them in specific tasks related to the business. He knew when shipments were coming in and how much was needed to supply the bartenders for weekly sales. He kept a running account of the transactions and had a talent for off-the-books book-keeping and numbers. He was the kind of guy that blended well into the background. Quiet and reserved, he didn't miss much and didn't make waves and always seemed to come through when needed. He even came and went at Bobby's private residence, working on financial reports and sometimes just hanging out. He wasn't a bother, didn't aggravate, didn't talk much, and took orders. Bobby knew little of his past except that he'd done time for a bookmaking scheme he'd been involved in. He didn't know that Keith was up to his eyeballs in debt due to his propensity for playing the numbers, had a connection to the Whalen Brothers through family ties, had been targeted by local law enforcement as a snitch, and was the last person Bobby suspected would "rat him out."

In the meantime, the DEA (Drug Enforcement Administration) had been contacted and the FBI brought in to begin an investigation of Bobby's activities. Local law enforcement came down hard on Keith and pressured him into making a deal, threatening him with arrest and exposure about the Whalen connection. He was up until then their most valuable resource. Keith was smart enough to realize that Bobby was about to be taken down and that it would be in his best interest to cooperate with the law. His loyalty was always swayed by the odds. He thought the odds were in his favor because there was no mafia syndicate ruling Asheville in association with Bobby to cause him to worry about a vendetta. Once Bobby was convicted, Keith believed he would be protected if he agreed to testify, that Bobby's arm wasn't as long as the arm of the law.

The DEA had unprecedented clout in the war on drugs. They were the agency responsible for enforcing the controlled substances laws and regulations of the United States. Agents were assigned to investigate and prepare for prosecution any known criminal or drug gang perpetrating violence in the community and terrorizing citizens through fear and intimidation. They managed their intelligence in cooperation with federal, state, and local officials to facilitate seizure and forfeiture of assets derived from, traceable to, or intended to be used for illicit drug trafficking. They also enforced the Controlled Substances Act as it pertained to the manufacture, distribution, and dispensing of legally produced controlled substances. Working with agents from the FBI, they started preparing arrest warrants for Bobby and his gang. They even brought in an explosives team because it had come to their attention that Bobby carried explosives, hand grenades in particular, and had a stockpile of weapons.

And then they went after Shelley. Keith let them know the extent of her involvement and that she was also Bobby's "Achilles' heel." They acted on this information by investigating every area of her life without her knowledge. Cautiously, they held back from arrest. Bobby was their main objective and they finally had enough evidence to move in on him and his entire operation.

It started to come down on a cold winter night, dark and bitter. Keith had been to the cabin that day, wearing a wire. Bobby hadn't noticed the thin layer of sweat that glistened on his forehead as he focused on his paperwork. He hadn't paid attention to Keith's nearby presence as he made a couple of buys over the phone and discussed a shipment of 2 kilos of cocaine that were to be delivered to the residence of one of the bartenders who worked at the Lone Dove named Twyla Webb. He'd waited until evening to head to her place to pick up the delivery. But when he got there and found out from her that it hadn't come, he was rattled.

Bobby drove back home, worried and unsettled. The next morning Twyla called and said she'd been contacted by UPS; the delivery had been delayed and would be there by late afternoon. He and Blaine returned, and were there when the package was left at her door. They waited. The days were short and the sun was setting. They waited until it was almost dark before opening the door and bringing the package inside. Blaine stood by as Bobby opened it. Inside was a stuffed animal, and inside of it instead of a kilo there was only one lousy 8-ball of cocaine.

Bobby looked at Blaine and said, "We're finished."

They looked toward the windows and saw blue-tinted light moving across the panes. They moved to the windows and looked out. Blue lights were flashing everywhere. It was an overkill sting operation and they didn't have a chance.

Blaine cocked his pistol, but Bobby held him back.

"Put it down, dude. Don't worry. We'll get out of it. We'll make bond."

But he would soon doubt his defiant words of bravado.

They took off their guns and stood in front of the picture window with their hands up in surrender. They gazed out upon a small army that looked like a militia surrounding them. The DEA and FBI agents appeared as a collective body. One of them stepped forward and announced, "Surrender and you'll be treated fairly," just as if they were in a war or combat zone.

Two heavily armed officers stormed in the door and put them in handcuffs.

As they were led away, the words "You'll be treated fairly," echoed in Bobby's mind; the statement seemed so amazing and strange. As he was driven away, separately from Blaine, in the caged-in back seat of a DEA sedan, it dawned on him in those dream-like moments of travel, winding along the narrow roads toward a new destiny, or perhaps the one to which he'd always been fated, that fairness was a concept he'd been grappling with since childhood, when the absence of it had driven him to complete despair. And now, powerless and captive, a man tells him that he'll be treated fairly. He wondered if such a thing was possible.

But another blow was to come, and it struck hard and sharp, like a knife piercing through his body and spirit. He found out they knew every detail of Shelley's involvement, and that she had been arrested when they'd raided his home and taken possession of his property and all of his assets. Despite their interrogations, she hadn't talked, even though they'd threatened her with money laundering and tax evasion charges. He knew this because they'd come back to him with a deal offer that would get her off the hook. The DEA wanted the rest of the cash, the bank locations, the lock box contents, all information that Kenny had not been able to supply.

Bobby willingly agreed to forfeit all his hidden bank cash if they would let her go. He had no choice. He loved her. But it would be the last thing he did for her. Once the deal was made, she dropped him. There were no visits, no letters, and no communication of any kind. The loss was incalculable. She was gone, his life seemed over, he had no alcohol to solace him and the craving for it clawed at his nerves. He felt restless and yet weary, wearing the look worn by animals in their first days of captivity, a bewildered mix of frantic and subdued, of being impossibly trapped with no means of escape. His adrenaline was depleted, his inner drive stalled. He was surrounded by misery, in a sordid cesspool of humanity, all of them locked together in a sickening system of punishment.

The realization hit him hard; he was too young for this. He'd grabbed at life with all the courage he could muster because, in truth, he'd loved it. Once he'd recovered from his illness and discovered a way to thrive and conquer, he'd gobbled up life like a starving child, taking what he wanted, savoring his power and possessions, hoarding away more than he'd ever need, and reveling in his escapades. And now, he was being held over the river again and no matter how he tried to writhe his way up and away from the frigid flowing waters, he was being pulled downward into a drowning pool as black as the mountainside that had shadowed his boyhood.

Then, out of the blue mountain mist, as if emerging from a dark cave, his father came to his aide like a big bear coming out of a long hibernation. He'd been awakened by the news and couldn't seem to grasp that his son had been arrested. He took it as a personal offense and it generated a surge of his old self, the still imposing stature and tidal force of his personality. Growling and plundering through the hallways, he thundered into the courthouse demanding justice, calling on favors with a threatening, cajoling mix of innuendo and persistence.

Bobby was at first surprised and then realized that his father's newfound vitality was aroused in part by the fact that he'd been taken down. When he'd felt powerful and had come swaggering into his parents home with plenty of money in his pockets, full of piss and vinegar and bravado during his visits, his father had acted disgruntled and appeared defeated and worn down. But now that he was once again powerless, incarcerated, and publically humiliated, his father was experiencing a revival, a reason to live, with a battle to fight and vengeance to be taken against old enemies and new.

Oh yes, Robert was in his element and exhilarated because it wasn't his life at stake. He could bluster and make people shudder and shake and throw his weight around and remind the big shots at city hall and the courthouse of their sordid pasts and mock the young bucks with their new law degrees and not worry about repercussions because it wasn't his ass on the line. And yet he made it appear that it was; his beloved son misjudged, falsely accused, caught by illegal entrapment, the drugs being planted and the weapons not relevant because they had been legally purchased. Truth was twisted, the argument unreasonable, the basis of fact incredible, and all with a cunning logic that made it appear that the entire raid had been a government plot against the rights of the common man. He ranted and railed and made people listen; he could have been the best defense attorney in the county if he'd chosen that profession as a young man.

While his father was shaking things up, which did create a

buzz around the legal community, Bobby was making a long-shot effort to establish contact with one of the best trial lawyers around, Sean Devereux. Bobby had heard of him and had requested through a phone call to his mother that she contact Devereux's office to implore him to take on the case. He hoped that his mother would be able to follow through. She was not doing well, but Bobby didn't realize the seriousness of her condition. Her health was deteriorating at about the same rate as her husband's escalating resurgence. It was almost too much for her to handle along with her son's arrest. But she rallied and came through, using her long years of work at the courthouse to make an impression on Devereux's secretary, who allowed her to get through to him and make her appeal. Although his schedule was full and his caseload heavy, he agreed to conduct an interview with Bobby at the Buncombe County Jail.

Sean Devereux was an unusual man, honorable and brilliant, an idealist, relatively young to have achieved his reputation, but he had because of his willingness to challenge controversy and defend those who created it. His roots were Irish, through and through. His father had been a leader and active member of Sinn Fein, Ireland's left wing Irish republican political party that, since forming in 1905, had historic ties to the Provisional IRA. Although his family had prospered in the United States after immigrating, the rebellious fight against oppression and injustice was instilled in him and from him into his son, Sean.

Sean was taught to understand that many people without guidance and leadership go about this fight in wrong ways. As a young attorney, he was attracted to such cases and developed the ability to ascertain the contributing factors which led to the actions of his clients and provide worthy defenses that significantly altered what would have ordinarily been dismal outcomes. He had taken on cases early in his law practice which some of his colleagues would have avoided like the plague. He'd defended Cherokee Indians with murder raps and controversial cases of notoriety, the most famous being Eric Rudolph, who had requested Sean after his arrest.

At the time of his arrest, Eric Rudolph had been on the FBI's Ten Most Wanted list, accused in the Centennial Olympic Park bombing in Atlanta. He'd spent more than five years hiding in the Appalachian wilderness as a fugitive during which federal and amateur search teams had scoured the area without success. It was believed that he had the assistance of sympathizers while evading capture and some were vocal about their support; two country songs were written about him. Sean was the first attorney appointed to his case until it was taken over by an attorney hired by Rudolph's controversial anti-abortion support system.

Sean Devereux was undecided about taking Bobby's case when he came to the Buncombe County Jail for the interview, thinking it a typical drug case. He had little time, an important case pending with the Court of Appeals under the Supreme Court, and was hesitant to take on another distraction. But there was something about Bobby's personality that captured his attention and interest and he couldn't put his finger on what it was.

It may have been the combination of vulnerability and toughness that Bobby revealed during their introduction. Bobby was so relieved to see him that he answered Devereux's questions as honestly and straightforwardly as possible, without denial, without excuses, and then proceeded to tell an earnest look-you-in-the-eye narrative that seemed genuine and surprisingly unique. He spent more time with Bobby than he'd planned, learned something of his life, and before he left, agreed to take the case.

Bobby was impressed with Sean from the beginning. He had the best of Irish good looks, a handsome man of medium height and weight with a soft smooth delivery and amicable personality. As they came to know each other better in the months to follow, Bobby learned that underneath his cool professional façade, Devereux was like a cocked gun waiting to go off when in defensive action, cunning and clever, and whiplash smart. In his personal life, he was a horseback rider and hunter, with a preference for hunting ring-necked pheasant. He was a devoted family man, even though he was known to have women falling all over him. His religious roots were Catholic, although he admitted that he didn't practice his faith as his father had. But his faith seemed to be as much a part of him as his Irish blood. He had a streak of rebellion in him that he held in reserve until it flared up in the defense of others, the same heritage that helped him to understand a miscreant like Bobby.

While Bobby was awaiting trial in the Buncombe County Jail, Sean came to know Robert, who loudly announced himself to Sean's secretary as "Mr. Robert Burris" and then bombarded his way into his office demanding to know how his money was being spent. The money in question was the money Bobby had transferred into his mother's account, which was being taken out in installments to pay for his defense. Robert had not only assumed ownership of the funds, he was trying to assume control of Bobby's life again, and by reclaiming control, thought he could give orders to his attorney.

During their first encounter, Sean was taken aback by the towering presence of the man. He'd been seated at his desk when Mr. Burris strode into his office, ignoring the secretary's attempt to escort him. Sean was still looking up at him even after standing, his hand swallowed up in the man's grip after he'd reached out to shake it. He'd felt intimidated by his physical strength and the threatening force of his personality. He'd not met anyone behind prison bars who had affected him this way, and he began to wonder about the effect Mr. Burris had had on his son, Bobby. It was not just the striking difference in their size. There were other distinct differences between this father and son that triggered Sean's curiosity about their relationship.

Bobby's father was a frightening and formidable man, different from others; there was something bestial about his manner. He brought to Sean's mind a story he'd read about a grizzly bear in a book he'd been given about the famous Lewis and Clark expedition. When he got home that night he took the book from its bookshelf and found it in one of the excerpts from their journals.

Lewis had recorded, "The men as well as ourselves are anxious to meet with some of these bear."

The Indians had given the white men "a very formidable account of the strength and ferocity of this animal." Lewis had discounted the information, although it did give him a bit of pause that the Indians, before attacking a grizzly, went through all the rituals they commonly used before going on a war party. Still, he and Clark and their men had faith that their long rifles were up to the task of taking one down. When Lewis and one of his men spotted two grizzlies barreling along the shore, they both shot and each man hit a bear. But one bear escaped and the other one charged at them for eighty yards and when it was finally put down they realized that, at over 300 pounds, it wasn't fully grown.

But even that didn't prepare them for the almost 600 pound grizzly that Clark later came upon and which Lewis described as "a most tremendous looking anamal, and extremely hard to kill notwithstanding he had five balls through his lungs and five others in various parts he swam more than half the distance across the river to a sandbar & it was at least twenty minutes before he died; he made the most tremendous roaring from the moment he was shot."

And the men stood awestruck by the sight and knowing that such creatures were roaming the lands along the river around them, they no longer wished to embrace the adventure of an encounter. Lewis wrote: "I find that the curiossity of our party is pretty well satisfyed with rispect to this animal."

And that awe matched the way Sean felt about Robert Burris, except that his curiosity wasn't satisfied. He wondered what it must have been like to be raised by such a man. He began to question Bobby about it and over the course of several visits Sean learned about his childhood and began to see the boy beneath the young man he was trying to defend. After their final interview, there was no more to be said and no reference to it to be spoken. Sean knew his client, understood him, and had become invested in him. Before he left the Buncombe County Jail that day, he called his secretary and asked her to clear the rest of his afternoon. He needed to clear his head of the images produced by Bobby's revelations.

Sean headed from Asheville to the Skyland Road exit and drove onto the road that snaked upward toward the Blue Ridge Parkway. Along the way, he thought about his own father, an imposing man in his own right, who had taught him wisely and well, and had set an outstanding example for him to emulate. He was a man with a big heart for his fellow man, except for the oppressors. He fought injustice like a mighty Angel of the Lord and rationalized his political ambitions as necessary. He'd raised his son to be a champion of his beliefs but made his beliefs seem commendable. Sean loved and respected his father and trembled at the thought of disappointing him. Sean thought about how different he might have been had his father been both impressive and unscrupulous and found it a confusing idea to consider.

Having reached the parkway, he drove along it slowly, looking to the side of the road where in some places there were sheer drop-offs only a few feet from the guard rail. He came to a semi-circled overlook parking area and stopped the car. He got out and walked to the center edge of the lot, beheld the vast panorama before him, and then looked downward at the solemn depths of the forest below. He stood for a time with intense concentration, peering into the deep green furrows that cut between the graduating ridges and highest peaks, as if he could see the hidden places in the valleys, gorges, hollows, crevices, coves and caves beneath them, and wondered at the secrets they held, the mysteries that remained unsolved. And then he raised his eyes and looked outward, taking in the graceful mounds of countless blue ridges disappearing into the distant horizon signifying an endless repeat of the landscape below him.

And then he silently questioned, "What manner of man could roam this wilderness and claim his right to it, making his own rules and ignoring those made by others, developing disdain for civil obedience and disregard for his fellow man, even his only son?"

There was nothing above him but powder-blue sky and cotton-white clouds. The air was still and the quiet soothing, a quiet impossible in the city. He thought of Robert Burris and what he had learned about him and what he had seen in him when they stood face to face, and he said aloud to no one but the mountains and the sky, "Jesus Christ, that son-of-a-bitch scares the shit out of me."

Sean drove back down the winding road from the parkway with a new sense of resolve. He would deal with Robert Burris and do everything in his power to give Bobby a solid defense.

Robert continued to be a nightmare to contend with and saved his winning charm for his old cronies, many of whom were still around. He reminded Sean regularly *who* he was dealing with, referring to Sean within earshot as a "piss-ant lawyer who still had a lot to learn." Sean's interactions with Burris paid off in the end, however, when he learned who was going to be the presiding judge over Bobby's criminal trial.

Judge Lacy Thornburg was an irascible personality and a member of the "old boy network" of a passing era. He had no use for drug dealers of any kind and was known for giving harsh sentences. But Sean had seen him surreptitiously talking to Robert Burris off to the side of the courthouse steps one afternoon and found out from Bobby about their long history of friendship dating back to their hunting buddy days. He suspected that Burris and Thornburg shared a few unspoken deeds of their own. Sean used this information to work out a deal, and convinced Robert Burris to back off, and he did it behind closed doors with the finesse of a diplomat and the strategy of a chess player.

There would be no trial. It was agreed that Bobby *had* to serve a sentence, but not the 10 to 20 years in a federal penitentiary he'd been facing. A trial would have resulted in certain conviction with the evidence the feds had against him. The deal had to appear to have merit. It was taken into account that Bobby had co-operated in giving over the money, a crucial factor in the sentence reduction, and his health record was unearthed to help determine where he would serve out the sentence. Sean Devereux had worked his magic. Bobby was sentenced to 6 years to be served in a Federal Medical Correctional Institution after being processed through the system, a punishing ordeal in itself.

When Bobby learned the news, he felt immense gratitude toward Sean Devereux and knew that he'd been given a chance for survival. Left alone in his cell, he fell to his knees and thanked the Lord he had forsaken for saving him from a future that would have kept him on the dark path for eternity. And although he didn't give himself over to the Lord at that time, a seed formed from his humble act of gratitude, rooted within him, and began to grow without his aid.

When his father heard the news, he had the opposite reaction. After having co-operated to some degree by backing off, he lunged forward again like the monstrous wounded bear he had defeated in his youth. Raised to his full height with claws bared, growling in rage, a wild look in his eyes, he vowed revenge. He blamed his old buddy Thornburg for punishing his son, blamed Sean Devereux for not getting him off, and blamed Bobby for betraying him by going out on his own and then getting caught. He blamed him just as he had years before when Bobby slashed the coach's tires. And worst of all, he blamed his wife for failing as a mother. It was the last blow she would endure and brought her to her end.

And still Robert ranted on and on. He blamed everyone but himself and then was left with himself, and then his self left him. It happened in a slow descent into dementia, and perhaps it had been there all along, causing the bouts of paranoia, fluctuating mood swings, distorted thinking, and fits of anger. And like the bear he had killed and the bear that Lewis had thought would never die, he fought to the end, which wouldn't come for many years.

CHAPTER FIFTEEN

A drunken man who falls out of a cart, though he may suffer, does not die. His bones are the same as other peoples', but he meets his accident in a different way. His spirit is in a condition of security. He is not conscious of riding in the cart; neither is he conscious of falling out of it. Ideas of life, death, fear, etc., cannot penetrate his breast; and so he does not fear from contact with objective existences. And if such security is to be got from wine, how much more is it to be got from God? It is in God that the Sage seeks his refuge, and so he is free from harm.
— Chuang Tzu 400 B.C.

Bobby's life seemed to have come full circle, from a time of youth and innocence to a time after the vision of his mother which left him feeling like a child again. He wanted to be a child in God's eyes, re-taught, reshaped, re-formed on the inside, and redeemed. Yet there he was, locked up in a prison, a medical institution, yes, but a prison just the same; acting as bodyguard for one of the most powerful crime bosses in the country, his roommates, "made men" who had cut their teeth within the criminal bowels of the New York underworld. It was an association that afforded some protection from the gangs of thieves and cutthroats that segregated the general inmate population and the psychos on the locked wards from which there was, hopefully, no escape possible.

Within his unit family, he had felt a bond of friendship and a safe haven of sorts that gave him the courage to make an attempt to be honest with Mickey Generoso about what was going on with him. He simply could not hide it anymore, not another month, not another week, not another day. It was impossible. The spirit that entered his soul during the vision was moving through him with an energy he could no longer contain. And it seemed to be working all around him, creating other strange happenings of late that seemed to fit in with his new purpose and desires.

An educational program had been introduced into the system sparking the interest of his boss, Mickey. Mickey had been schooled in many things and was a very wise man, but as a child had never had the luxury of a formal education and had disguised for years the fact that his reading abilities were minimal. He decided on his eightieth birthday to enroll in the reading classes within the program and work toward obtaining a GED. He had less than a year left of his sentence and had been eager to start classes that week. This provided Bobby with a window of opportunity, two hours each morning, to study the Bible he'd taken out of the library. He told Mickey of his intentions and shared with him in private what he'd experienced, assuring him that in every other respect he would perform his duties and remain the same.

The morning he began reading the Bible, Dominick was there due to a schedule change in his job assignment. When he saw the Bible in Bobby's hands, he began to ridicule him and continued to needle him off and on all morning. Johnny G was gone that morning doing maintenance, so Dominick felt free to be more obnoxious than usual. Bobby tried to ignore him as he began what would become a habit of daily reading.

When Dominick told Johnny G about it, he had a different reaction. He was a "live and let live" kind of guy, unless provoked. But Dominick had a cruel side and it irritated him that Bobby was into what he called "this religious bull." Living with Dominick in such close quarters was a strain. Dominick could be mean-spirited, was always in a bad mood, angry and bitter about having to serve time, and often lashing out when Mickey wasn't around.

One morning, class had been cancelled and Mickey was there and so was Johnny G. Bobby had by this time been forthright with both of them about his conversion and desire to change. He'd assured them that his bodyguard job would continue un-affected because he believed it to be a righteous job in the cir-cumstances in which they lived. He requested only the time he was not needed to pursue his Bible studies, and they had not objected. This had irritated Dominick even more and that morn-ing he blurted out without thinking,

"Why do you read that damned Bible? If there really is a God, how come he doesn't get you out?"

Bobby had had enough and stood up. In prison, when a man stands up to face an adversary, it means he is ready to go to an-other level.

"You want to read all your crazy books about gambling to help you run your games when you get out. I'm going to read the book that will help me."

Dominick rose from where he was sitting and Mickey and Johnny G turned their attention to him. They knew what he was capable of and had seen him in action on the outside. Dominick's mean streak was lit a-fire and a dangerous confrontation was about to begin.

It happened like a streak of lightening. Mickey crossed the room and took Dominick by the collar and swung him around to face him.

"That kid can read the Bible when he wants to and where he wants to and you keep your mouth shut or you're out of here!"

Dominick seemed to shrink before Mickey's black-eyed glare of scorn and slinked back to his bunk. Johnny G grinned almost imperceptibly and gave Bobby a slight nod. Dominick said noth-ing more for the remainder of the day.

Bobby's step out about his intentions had brought about an unexpected result. Mickey had given him his blessing and there-fore he had the protection he'd needed to go forward in the de-velopment of his faith. And in a strange way it would have a pos-itive effect on everyone in the cell, including Dominick. For one thing, he kept his mouth shut and his persistent grumbling had come to a halt. The atmosphere in the large room lightened and a quiet harmony ensued. Johnny G, who had a sense of humor, expressed it more often and Mickey even talked about his progress at prison school. It was really incredible that something like this could blossom between prison walls, between men who terrified most of the other inmates when not in their cocoon.

Bobby wondered how things would change after Mickey's release. But that was months away and he tried to make the most of his morning routine. There was also another routine that was followed each morning, the "making of the gravy." Gravy was the term used for the sauce that he and Johnny G would start in the morning in preparation for the later meals. The sauce was made with ingredients supplied by the kitchen for the dinners that Mickey was accustomed to eating on the outside. The only difference in the cooking was that it had to be done in a microwave oven and the sauce stirred every few minutes until done. Dominick had found other duties to perform during the morning hours and Bobby enjoyed this private time with Johnny G and the opportunity to get to know him better.

Johnny G, or "G" as they sometimes called him, was the exact opposite of Dominick. He was a man who never complained. No matter how he felt physically or in any other respect, when asked how he was doing or how he felt, he'd always reply, "Great!" If he heard bad news from home or something disturbing regarding his legal problems, it never bled over into the day-to-day life on the unit.

And he stood out amongst everyone there, like a movie star does from the crowd. Bobby thought G carried himself like a man should; he was impressive and yet quiet about it. He was in his mid-fifties, with amazingly thick black hair, an olive complexion, good-looking and in excellent shape, considering he had a history of hepatitis, a health condition he'd managed successfully for years. He watched what he ate, worked out every day on the weight pile, and loved to get out in the sun whenever possible, which kept him looking tan and healthy. He was able to do this while working beyond their unit doing maintenance, mostly painting, for the over-all Units Staff Manager, Miss Lynch. Miss Lynch looked like one of those sturdy uniformed women depicted in Cold War propaganda photos of Russia. She had access to his files and knew that he'd made it to the upper echelon of the mob. She was both impressed and intrigued by him and assigned what she called her "honey-do list" which kept him in attendance without crossing any barriers that would jeopardize her position. She just loved to look at him and have him at her beck and call, and he took full advantage of it in his laid back way. He painted both interior and exterior walls of the units, which gave him more time in the outdoors than most of the inmates had.

Johnny never talked about himself and Bobby hesitated to question him about anything personal. Some inmates talked about their "big shit past" like it was a badge of honor and others bragged about things that they should have kept secret. The place was full of low-life losers who had started as street punks, become gang members for life, and had expected to die young leaving behind a history of mayhem. Instead, due to gunshot wounds, injuries from beatings, stabbings, and being maimed from other forms of abuse, addiction problems and residual effects from drug overdoses, they'd been sentenced to a place where they tried to re-establish the same lifestyle they lived on the outside.

The gang affiliations that proliferated in other prisons could not compare to ones in a federal medical correctional institution where their members were a walking testament to the cost of these lifestyles. They didn't have to talk; it was written all over them and many were half-crazy in the bargain. And yet they, too, told their tales of horror and got off on outdoing each other in describing gruesome feats of brutality. They made a guy like Johnny G seem like a captured dark knight being held in a defeated kingdom that existed in a time from the Middle Ages. And he made Bobby feel like one of his musketeers when he started to take an interest in him. At least that was the way Bobby liked to think about it, having always had a creative imagination.

Bobby admired Johnny G and imagined the many dragons he must have slain as a "made man" under Paul Castellano, boss of the Gambino family. It was like he had an invisible boundary around him that kept people at a distance without making them feel offended by it. He was a good listener, too, and when Bobby remarked on it, Johnny replied, "Maurice Chevalier used to say that the greatest conversationalist is the best listener."

And then he told him more about the man, his long career on the stage and in the movies beginning in the 1930s. "He'd been nothing but a poor street kid in France and then ended up an unofficial ambassador between the U.S. and France, just because he had charm."

Johnny liked Chevalier's music, which Bobby found odd, since it wasn't Italian or sung by Sinatra. And so it was that they cooked the sauce together and talked about unlikely and inconsequential things and Johnny listened, and then Bobby started to share more and more about himself. What had started with his revelations to Sean Devereux came forth from him as naturally as water flowing from a stream. Johnny made it easy, asking lots of questions, particularly about his time in the freemasons and the secret nature of the organization. He told Bobby he respected any man who could keep a secret, or a group of men that could share a secret and keep it, which he believed to be much harder.

He said, "A secret is like a bond, kid. It's not meant to be held over someone like a club or used as a weapon. Then it becomes something else, a threat, and must be dealt with like any threat. That kind of secret holds no honor and that kind of bond is meant to be broken."

Bobby was shaken by these words because he had lived them, and they freed him even more to talk about things that for so many years he had been forced to hide. And it was perhaps made easier by the fact that his secrets were less shocking to a man with Johnny's history, whatever that might be. Johnny was an enigma to Bobby, mysterious and complex, and when he did reveal something, it seemed out of left field and from another area of interest that always disrupted Bobby's preconceived notions about him.

The rest of his waking hours were devoted to Mickey. Faith aside, he had to get through his time and Mickey was second in his mind only to God. He waited on him and served him and kept the fruit bin stockpiled and the wolves outside at bay. Mickey had a great appetite for his age and the preparation of his food was as important as each mealtime. He expected all the amenities, or as many as could be acquired in their Spartan surroundings. It was a ritual of life, ingrained in him since childhood. In the morning it was fruit and grains, at the dinner hour, pasta and whatever meat or fish was available with, of course, the "gravy."

One morning during this time, Bobby was preparing an orange for Mickey's breakfast. They'd obtained a bag of fresh Florida oranges the day before. After he peeled and sectioned it into small pieces and placed it before Mickey, he prepared two more for Johnny G and Dominick and then went back to the counter to clean up the mess and while doing so reached into the bin for another one for himself. But he didn't take the time to cut the orange into small sections; he broke it into quarters instead and popped one of them into his mouth. While chewing it he swallowed too quickly and the orange section lodged in his throat and he started to choke. He couldn't breathe and was turning blue and the three men pushed their chairs back from the table and stood up and watched in shock and horror as he gasped for breath and started losing consciousness.

Mickey suddenly shouted, "The kid's dying, do something!"

Johnny lurched forward and grabbed Bobby from behind and did a Heimlich maneuver on him and the piece of orange popped back out and onto the floor.

He pulled over a chair and helped Bobby into it and then the three men stood there looking at him until Mickey quietly looked at Johnny G and said, "You saved his life, G. You know what that means?"

Bobby couldn't look up. He felt sick and embarrassed and relieved to be alive and was now waiting to hear what unimaginable consequence might follow.

Johnny G replied with resignation, "Yeah, I know."

And then he looked at Bobby and said, "It means I saved your life, kid. I'm responsible for you now. You belong to me."

He looked up at Johnny G in astonishment, but his internal reaction was visceral, taking him back in time like a movie reel spinning backwards out of control. He only knew one meaning of belonging to someone and it wasn't good. Would he now be a pawn, a chess piece of lowest value to be played at Johnny's whim, to be used for more wet work and other evil deeds? Would the soul he was trying to salvage be held hostage once again and blackened for good? Would the life he was hoping to own one day be controlled to the end of his days by a Gambino mob guy?

All of his progress with Johnny was forgotten in the seconds it took for him to be transported back to a place of mistrust. What the hell were they talking about and what did it mean?

Who and what was this Johnny G under his smooth persona? He hadn't become "made" because of his charm, like a Chevalier. Was Mickey the reason some of the meanest assholes on the unit backed away when Johnny G walked by, or was it he alone who inspired such fear and respect? The questions streamed through his mind as their eyes were upon him and he couldn't respond, couldn't speak a word. Thankfully, they attributed his silence to a constricted throat.

Surprisingly, his fears were unfounded and from that day forward Johnny G took Bobby under his wing, rather than taking over his life. Thus, Bobby came to know him better and learned a little more about his history. Johnny was in prison for an Interstate Transportation of a Gambling Device conviction, for not having the proper gambling stamp attached to poker machines that were set up in truck stops throughout Louisiana. Prior to his arrest, he'd been sent to New Orleans by Castellano to oversee gambling device distribution in the city and surrounding areas. His criminal history also included work with the unions; Johnny had a knack for insuring that things ran smoothly, so perhaps charm did have something to do with his position in the mob, and diplomacy.

He was a man of many interests, and one of them was hunting; he was interested in learning to cook wild game and they had many lengthy talks on these subjects. His discussions with Bobby were fatherly and almost affectionate. Bobby started to relax around him, felt calmer, like he'd been taken off a high wire act and could now work steady on the ground. He began to trust again that something was happening that he'd always needed, that it wouldn't change in an instant and be taken away just as he'd come to depend on it. And he found in this man, whom he had doubted, a father figure who rose to the occasion and seemed to also accept it as his purpose. Bobby could see nothing bad in this man and erased from his mind any aspect of Johnny G's life or past that swayed him from looking up to him as an example.

And in the process of studying his Bible and experiencing the most stable environment he had ever known, ironically within his unit cell, he began to have ideas about life which he had not previously considered. He thought that all men had within them the capacity for good and evil. He visualized a spectrum that stretched out like a long line on which at one end the most extreme of evil was shadowed in darkness and at the other the most extreme of good was bathed in light, the center being a midway point between the two. He saw both ends leading straight into eternity. He saw human beings being pulled in both directions by circumstances, influences, and the events of life, and struggling to stay somewhere in the middle. Those closer to the extreme of each end were probably not going to turn back, the distance being too great and the pull at each end like the pull of gravity. He knew that he'd come dangerously close to being sucked into the dark end for all of eternity and was taking the long stretch of highway back toward the light. He saw the men around him making the same effort, each of them at different places on the spectrum, some maybe closer to the darkness than he knew.

But he did know one thing. There were miracles that could help a person change direction, and if a person was lucky enough to have one, he had to be willing to do the work to stay on course and not turn back. It might be the only chance, the only miracle, the only time in life that an intervening phenomenon occurred, and he'd had more than one. He'd survived the illness, the illness had brought him to the institution, the vision had visited him in the unit, and the approval he had always needed was around him there like a nurturing balm.

Something was happening within that unit cell that was having an effect on each of its inhabitants, and for that he felt blessed and grateful. He wondered at God's mercy and capacity for forgiveness, and questioned his worthiness for such gifts. Then he remembered a gospel saying that old Jed had repeated, one that had irritated him because he didn't understand it. He decided to look it up and found it in Romans, 5th Chapter, 20th and 21st verses:

> "Moreover, the law entered, that the offense might abound. But where sin abounded grace did much more abound. That as sin hath reigned unto death, ever, so might grace reign through righteousness to eternal life by Jesus Christ our Lord."

He thought, yes, the law entered my life and my sins became apparent to me and maybe through my mother's intervention, coming to me in the vision, I received grace; not because I'd earned it, but because of what I might do with it from now on. Bobby took it to mean that God had put some faith in him instead of the other way around and had given him a chance to stay on a life path that would save his eternal soul. He could have had another fate, evidence of that was all around him, every time he escorted Mickey out the door, down the hallways, into the yard, everywhere the dark end of the spectrum had its pull, and in this place it was working overtime.

CHAPTER SIXTEEN

In the end, it is our defiance that redeems us. If wolves had a religion—if there was a religion of the wolf—that is what it would tell us.
— *Mark Rowlands*, The Philosopher and the Wolf

Bobby might have been a "kid" in the eyes of Mickey Generoso, and perhaps even Johnny G, but he was in his thirties and after Mickey's release would be facing three more years in prison. In two and a half more years, Johnny would be released and then he'd be on his own. Serving time was hard and fraught with challenges. The unit population changed with every incoming felon and some of them weren't afraid of anything. The traditional mafia had little meaning to younger hotshots trying to impress their gang members, until they were educated by warnings or an experience with one of them.

One afternoon, Bobby, Johnny G, and Dominick were in the yard talking to Richie Fusco, a high ranking captain in the Colombo family. Richie was Johnny's cousin by marriage and they were close despite having different mob affiliations. No one messed with Fusco. Unlike Johnny G, Richie's reputation for violence was well-known, hair-trigger, and could be easily directed into threatening offensive action, a trait that had been valued by his boss. Richie had a fondness for Johnny G and that alone gave Johnny extra clout on the unit. Bobby's mistaken assumption about Johnny's past in the immediate aftermath of the orange incident had been cleared up in his mind and he'd come to know why Richie was far more threatening. He'd seen several incidents involving Richie but one in particular stood out.

The White Supremacist skin-head gangs had multiplied on the units. They usually stayed to themselves when out in the yard, plotting their moves against the black militant gangs who kept them at bay with their own brand of muscle. But one young punk boss hadn't given Richie Fusco what he considered proper respect and had even spit in his direction in front of the others, trying to prove something, like a Bantam rooster trying to appear bigger than he is. This rooster decided to walk across the yard one day into Richie's territory as if to dare him into an exchange. Richie called him over and put his arm around his neck and whispered something into his ear. When he was through, he pushed him away and the young skin-headed boss looked pale and sick. As he walked away, Richie said aloud to him, "You'd better remember that to me you are nothing but something sticky on my shoe. You are nothing."

He must have remembered because it didn't happen again, respect was paid, and whatever Richie had whispered was believed and taken seriously.

Power struggles were common in the yard. When things got too peaceful, something had to be stirred up; it could be felt like an undercurrent running beneath the yard. Aggressions had to be released and frustrations expressed. But there was a fine line that could not be crossed or the recreation time would be taken away and the alternative was a worse hell; total confinement. One such incident had occurred during the previous week. An altercation began when a huge black inmate with arms the size of melons continued to monopolize the weights. The weight pile had to be used in turn and there were not enough weights to accommodate the number of men who wanted to work out. A scrawny member of one of the Mexican gangs confronted him and was ignored. He spent that night working on a plastic rounded knife that he had smuggled from the mess hall, broke the tip off, ground and sharpened it, and taped it to the palm of his hand and fingers to give it more strength and support. The next day in the lunch line, he walked up behind the large man and leaped onto his back, proceeding to stab the knife into his neck again and again and again until he was over-taken by the guards and taken away. The incident resulted in a shut-down that lasted two days, loss of recreation time and privileges for everyone.

Since then, tensions had been running high in the yard. As they stood there talking to Richie, they were alerted by the sound of raised voices coming from the other side of the yard near the weight pile. Richie turned from facing them and looked in the direction of the commotion and then scanned the yard. Whatever had flared up had just as quickly subsided. Richie looked back at Bobby and Johnny, rubbing the left temple of his forehead and wincing, an incredulous expression on his face.

He said, "It's a different world out there, man. These bastards are so messed up it's like we're living on another god-dammed planet. And, they're getting crazier every day."

Bobby had to agree. Things were changing. He decided to heed Richie's words and re-assess his surroundings in order to better protect Mickey, and himself. He'd been living too much in his head of late and needed to take a good look around and reevaluate the order of things. The Kentucky facility had in the past few years restructured their drug addiction program to work in accordance with a new judicial concept called "Drug Courts." Offenders convicted of drug charges in Drug Court were often mandated to federal institutions with addiction programs if they met the criteria. Alcohol and other drug dependence had been deemed a medical condition recognized by the American Medical Association and, as such, met one of the criteria for placement in a federal medical correctional institution. Other criteria included a minimal conviction record, which did not take into account felons with dangerous criminal histories who had only been convicted once or twice, another being a record of cooperation with the feds. This added to the unit population inmates who could be physically healthy except for drug dependence — who were often more dangerous because of it, and brought in new groups of offenders linked to South American syndicates and drug cartels that had established permanent residence in the United States.

One of the most dangerous recent additions had been a Jamaican gang leader by the name of Vivian Blakely. Since his transfer to the facility, he'd been causing a new wave of disturbance throughout the units and upsetting the ever unsteady balance and changing pecking order of the already established Jamaican and Cuban gangs. Blakely hailed from the Caribbean Island of St. Croix and also owned a private island separate from any real country. He'd operated from this island, competing with Jamaican rivals and Cuban gangs, with whom he'd had lots of trouble. Several of their members were represented on the units. Most of them had ratted to help the feds and there was much hatred and distrust between them. Blakely quickly consolidated the Jamaicans, putting aside his grievances, at least for a time, because he hated the Cubans even more. Once he formed his Jamaican gang, he ran it like a tribal king and the retaliations against the Cubans began soon after, with little regard for collateral damage. Even the Colombian cartel gangs steered clear of this bunch.

There were three Central American Colombian factions represented on the units: the Cali Cartel, Pablo Escobar's group, and the Black Tuna Gang. They were also linked to MASA, the Mexican Syndicate (MS) and Spanish syndicate gangs. These groups didn't get along at all with the black militant gangs, which were represented by the Bloods, the Cripps (Community Revolution in Progress) from L.A, and the Gangster Disciples from Chicago.

The tightest group and the most sinister were the Chinese gangs. There were several represented; the Green Dragons were the most ruthless. Although separated into sects, they would all stick together, never talked, never ratted, and if you messed with one, you had all of them to contend with and they'd beat or stab you to death for just trying.

Then there were the biker gangs, made up of members of the Hell's Angels and the Outlaws. And the White Supremacists, the skin-heads, the Arian Brotherhood, the New SS, their main adversary being the militant black gangs.

The sects that created the most controversy on the units were the American Indians, the Native Americans; the older tribe members still referred to themselves as Indians. They stuck together, too; basically all lived under one tent, except for the Oglala Sioux from Nebraska and the Dakotas; they hated everybody, particularly the "wachitcha" the white man. Some were from the Wounded Knee area; they didn't mix, and would only speak English when they had to. But they would participate in the sweat lodge.

The tribes had petitioned and filed lawsuits to have special worship that included having sweat lodge meetings and permission to use tobacco for their spiritual ceremonies, the tobacco provided by the institution. Many guys on the unit started claiming to have Indian blood so they could get in on the sweat lodge ceremony and have free tobacco. The Sioux leaders got mad about the intruders and complained, resulting in a new rule that anyone participating in the ceremony had to attend six weeks of study and worship, resolving the problem.

And in the midst of all this, there was a temporary conflict involving the Irish Republican Army (IRA) group and a member of the Ulster Defense Fund (UDF), the direct opposite of the IRA and a protestant pro-England organization. Prison officials made a decision they later regretted by putting these two factions in the same facility, hoping they would form a truce like the mafia and other factions had done. But when the first UDF prisoner arrived, it became evident that this was not going to happen. This guy had been arrested for an armed car robbery, been convicted, and was reputed to have sent a hit squad to take out the Federal judge who had sentenced him. He was a braggart and a loud mouth who expressed openly his hatred for Catholics, stating that "The only Catholics that got into his car were dead ones."

"Getting in a car" in prison jargon meant getting in with a group or doing something with someone.

So he offended the Catholic mob guys as much as he did the IRA members. And then he threatened a guard for taking him out of the lunch line for wearing improper prison attire, stating, "You think you're tough. You should be careful, I've got long arms. If you put me in the hole, I'll get your family."

The guard hit the panic button on his radio that sent off a signal to the captain's office and a 10-man squad, the prison emergency response team, known as the "goon squad" by the prisoners, took him away, with him screaming all the way. That was the end of him.

Bobby came to the conclusion that the bullying and blustering, the bragging and the bluffing, the mouthing off that went on day after day, were the catalyst to most of the outbreaks of violence. They were acts of aggression and defiance that he understood well. He'd done it himself in his own way, like a stage actor who had memorized a script for survival, play-acting in the criminal world with all the flair he could muster. He'd had none of these defenses when he was young; his attempts at defiance had resulted in severe punishment and crushing defeat. It had taken him years to hone an act that finally enabled him to overcome his feelings of powerlessness. This act seemed nothing more than a shell to him now, and for the first time in his life he'd become still and quiet inside. However, he also had to get through this "valley of the shadow of death" and wear the shell for just a little while longer.

Taking time to consider his situation one morning, another voice intruded upon his reverie, that of old Jed. This time it was one of the proverbs Jed had repeated so many times that Bobby knew it by heart, Proverb 18:21, only this time, he finally understood its meaning.

"Death and life are in the power of the tongue and they that love it shall eat the fruit thereof."

From that point on, Bobby guarded his speech and never spoke his mind unless in the private company of Mickey and Johnny. In the months before this, he'd poured everything out to Johnny G about himself. In the months that followed, he listened more than he talked. They had deep and meaningful conversations that fueled his thirst for knowledge and set his imagination and natural curiosity ablaze. The camaraderie within their small group continued as they each prepared for Mickey's departure in their own way.

There had been many visits from the outside; Mickey met with subordinates who brought messages from his underboss, emissaries from other families visited, his special counsel and other attorneys, plans were being made in many quarters. Mickey took care of business on the inside, too, bestowing gifts on those who had ensured his privileges.

Johnny G would now take over his position in their quarters until his release, scheduled for six months prior to Bobby's release. Johnny might not have Mickey's aura, but he had enough to maintain the status quo of their living arrangements and it would be up to him who would be chosen to move in with them. And since Dominick was also a Gambino member, it was likely that another one would join them. Bobby had some reservations about this but felt confident that he could serve out the next three years, staying on course, because of his relationship with Johnny G. He didn't like to think about what his time there might have been like had Mickey not taken him in.

Mickey received his GED certificate one week before his release. They gave him a small graduation ceremony to celebrate his accomplishment and a big send-off party. He chose that occasion to have a talk with Bobby about his future. The old man seemed younger that day than he had on the day of their first meeting. Since that time, he'd witnessed Mickey assume mob family leadership, give orders and make decisions and conduct business from a locked down unit in a federal institution. He could only imagine the power he would wield on the outside, the acknowledgement of that power awaiting him in a ceremony that had been in preparation for months. There were times when Bobby wondered if the old man would still be alive when he got out. That day, he had no doubt about it because he could see the years left in Mickey's eyes and physical bearing, and the transformation that had come over him when handed the piece of paper that was equivalent to a high-school diploma. He would be a force to be reckoned with in his eighties and Bobby knew that Mickey's course had been determined a long time ago. They were heading in different directions.

Mickey told him that an unofficial position would be waiting for him upon his release, that he could have the option of New York or Florida as a home base, with regular visits to the mountains, and that his position would be unchallenged and an arrangement would be worked out to ensure this. It was an unprecedented offer, but he had no illusions about the moral choice he was about to make.

He looked straight into Mickey's eyes and spoke directly to him with honesty and sincerity, but it was also in a peaceful, quiet way, a momentous act of defiance.

"While you're here, Mickey, I'm with you mind, body, and, spirit. But when I get out, my life is the Lord."

Mickey looked at him with the fondness a grandfather might have for a favored grandson and said, "Well, just in case, I'll keep an eye on you until you do get out, and when you do, if you change your mind, the job is yours."

Mickey had more faith in the nature of man than he did in man's faith in God. During his lifetime, he'd seen too many war trench conversions and believed them to be a temporary condition, that "a leopard can't change his spots."

His war trenches had been the mean streets of Prohibition era New York during his childhood, the gangster wars dating back to his early days as a mafia soldier, the glory days in Cuba, when he'd gambled with Duke Ellington and other show business luminaries like Nat King Cole who entertained at the Havana casinos, George Raft who greeted the guests with his movie star gangster appeal, and a young Frank Sinatra who was also brought in to perform.

He'd witnessed meetings with Fulgencio Batista Zaldivar, the Cuban President, dictator, and military leader who served as the leader of Cuba and who collaborated with the heads of the five mafia families, taking regular kickbacks from the lucrative casino profits which were delivered on a weekly basis by their bag men. He'd stayed in extravagant casino hotels that were monuments to the gambling, vice, and corruption primarily supported by rich Americans and a Hollywood elite who flocked there regularly to share in the fantasy spoils. It was a time when heroin and cocaine operations were run from Havana, making Cuba the great way station for the drug trade; the mafia funded airline companies to transport the drugs. Lucky Luciano was the king of Havana and Cuba was the center of the mob universe. Millions were being made from the casinos and the drug trade but the Cuban people were not benefitting at all from the profits.

Mickey had watched as the mob bosses and Batista turned a blind eye to what was happening around them, in the streets and out in the countryside, where rebel forces had been organized by a strong and charismatic leader. In the casinos it seemed as though the party would last forever, until the fateful New Year's Eve of 1958 when Fidel Castro led the revolution to overthrow the Cuban government. And from that experience he had learned to look beyond any enclosed group or environment to the bigger picture of human behavior to gauge his decisions and his choices. He had learned a great deal about rebellion in that year of 1959 and part of the wisdom he gained was to never underestimate his fellow man, no matter how over-powered or downtrodden. He had recognized a similar rebellious spirit in Bobby, but his rebellion had been growing against the life he'd been living, the life he'd been brought up to live. Nevertheless, Mickey couldn't help but remain skeptical, believing that men seldom changed, even when their lives were changed for them.

He'd seen the revolution change the fortunes of syndicate bosses who'd invested heavily in Cuban real estate and casinos, and then watched them redirect their investments into takeovers in Las Vegas and Los Angeles during the heyday of the Hollywood movie industry. He'd met the likes of Joe Kennedy, who also had investments there and later used his mob connections to help get his son elected President of the United States; following in his father's footsteps, his son used a more experienced Frank Sinatra to make Hollywood connections and help him raise campaign funds, only to drop him after becoming President because of his ties to the mafia.

He'd observed every type of hypocrisy, disloyalty, and betrayal, and dealt with crooked union bosses and corrupt politicians, fraudulent legitimate businessmen, and dishonest cops. He'd seen the good and bad in men inside and outside of the law and had no illusions about his place in the scheme of things, but he did believe in God, had his own sense of integrity, and knew that he would work it out with his Maker in the end. He'd accepted his way of life from the beginning, as though it had been destined. Perhaps Bobby could change his destiny, but still Mickey doubted.

He'd lived through the power wars within and between the five families, the vendettas and necessary decisions over life and death, and had seen men who were doomed to die pray to God for help, mercy, and for life in their final moments "under the gun," promising anything. And in those cases when life had been given back as a reprieve, most reverted to the actions that had led them to death's door in the first place; the God to whom they had prayed and made promises was forgotten once more.

He'd seen convicted felons converting to religion, carrying

on about being saved, using it at their parole hearings, only to be denied because no one on the parole board had faith in them either. He figured that most would return to criminal life as soon as they were released because he knew that life on the outside was not changed because someone on the inside had changed. Although he saw Bobby as different from the rest, and had developed great affection for him, he'd been around too long to put a lot of money on a long shot without hedging his bets. He'd also grown accustomed to having Bobby around and knew he would miss him. The kid had balls; that was for sure. If he did revert to his old ways, Mickey wanted him back by his side.

But the rebellious spirit that he saw in Bobby was stronger than Mickey realized, strengthened by his deep mountain roots and bred into him like his love for the wild forest and the freedom it offered.

He was a mountain rebel, through and through, only this time his rebel cry had meaning and he was fighting for the noble cause that had brought about his salvation.

CHAPTER SEVENTEEN

Go at once, this very minute, stand at the cross-roads, bow down, first kiss the earth which you have defiled, and then bow down to all the world and say to all men aloud, "I am a murderer!" Then God will send you life again. Will you go, will you go?
— Fyodor Dostoevsky, Crime and Punishment

Bobby's rebellion started with his respectful rejection of Mickey's offer. But he had much to think about before he could take it any further. After Mickey was gone, he had more time to reflect upon his wrongdoings. He fell to his knees in deep remorse over his sins against God and man. He felt disconnected from the person who had committed the acts he confessed and knew in his heart that he would not commit them again. The grace he'd been given had taken away from him all evil intent. He did not understand why he had been chosen for such a gift. And he cried for those he had harmed and for the mercy he'd received.

He came to believe that no amount of time in prison could make up for his crimes, not even a lethal injection. He came to the realization that by giving his life over to the Lord, the man he had been in the past had been executed by the grace of God and that the shell he was living in, the one that looked like tough-acting Bo-Guns Burris, would be left behind upon his release to parole, like a shell of a dead snail.

He'd come to the crossroads of his life and the road he was about to take was a great unknown. He knew that Mickey had doubts about his decision to go straight and he didn't blame him for thinking that way. Most people would, and he'd given this quite a bit of thought.

Some of the guys he was serving time with had every intention of repeating their crimes after release, educating themselves in their area of expertise, devising plans and plotting strategies, going over and over in their heads where they had made their mistakes, how these mistakes could be avoided next time, who would be in on the job, who would be taken care of for ratting on them, gaining-entry plans and get-away plans, reconnecting and regrouping, hitting the mark, making that final big score. Others kept their intentions to themselves, their insidious plans, prurient acts of deviance, perversion and madness.

Many were just trying to do their time, treading the middle of the road, the median of the line, not making promises, not expecting dramatic change, just trying to get through, and then make it through parole. There were those who were desperate to change, to stay off drugs, to reunite with their families, to begin a new life; most of them kept quiet about it and many lost their resolve; some were broken by the system, defeated before they began. The guys with the best chances were those with something to hope for, something to believe in outside the life that had pulled them down. There had to be something burning inside a man to keep him hanging in there and Bobby thought he knew what it was inside of him.

He'd heard a lot of talk about making choices since his arrest, both good choices and bad, that your life was governed by the choices you made. But looking back, he didn't believe he had chosen the life of a criminal, not really. Oh later, yes, maybe he did, or maybe he just thought he had. It was hard for him to determine when the line was drawn between his choices and his father's. Because always his father had been there, influencing his actions, dominating his life. He wasn't trying to make excuses; he was just trying to figure out where Robert Burris left off and where Bobby Burris began.

When he'd been small, a little boy, he'd known love and tenderness. His grandmother had taught him to believe in a God of greatness and watchfulness. He'd been afraid of that God, but she hadn't been. She talked about the good Lord all the time and spoke of him with admiration and respect. He remembered wanting to please that God, wanting to be a good boy, desiring it just as he'd wanted to please his grandmother so that he could feel her warm praise and then feel it again in his stomach when he ate the fluffy biscuits she made for him "for being such a thoughtful boy." How he loved bringing her things from the forest, and that one day, a wild turkey, how he'd basked in her love and affection, "her little renegade heathen." He understood why his grandfather loved her so much. Grandpa Stanton also prayed to the Lord, and they had both gone to be with him in death, Bobby believed that.

But all of that love and tenderness would evaporate when he'd return home to the other side of the mountain, to the darkness, the black side of the mountain where his father taught him to do wrong and make it seem like it was a normal way to live. Instinctively, he'd known that it wasn't normal, every time he had to be involved in an act of destruction helping his Dad get back at someone. And then he'd been used to aid in the murder of CB. He'd suffered deeply for it, suffered as deep as any grown man might who believed he'd committed murder, murder of a good man, a man who had liked him and thought he was a good boy. He'd suffered because he had a conscience then and believed himself to be a murderer and went through the hell of nightmares and stomach pains and guilt that ate away at him until he finally found a way to relieve it. And he'd suffered in silence, with no one to talk to and no one to tell him that he wasn't responsible for what happened. He'd even convinced himself that he had known it would happen, had seen it in his father's eyes and didn't warn CB, and the guilt was compounded until he'd felt so bad about himself, so awful inside that he felt he wasn't worth anything. And that was the murder for which he'd been truly punished, because it cost him his childhood and led to words spoken to his father that almost got him killed.

When he'd said those words, his one attempt at rebellion, he was nearly drowned, terrorized and thrown to the corner of a boat like a worthless wet rag. And still he had tried to please the man and it was never enough. His father made him feel that he was never good enough, never smart enough, until he finally found a way to get his attention, and gain his approval; and the only way to do that was to do things his way, obey him, try to be like him, prove himself worthy through wicked acts of destruction and violence, helping him spit in the face of authority, being nothing more than a puppet he held by the strings. And all the while he'd tried to convince himself that he was becoming his own man by these actions and others done with his gang unbeknownst to his father. But all of it was done with the same aim, he could see that now. It was all an effort to gain his father's love and respect. But respect for what?

What were those father and son trips to the coast all about? Year after year, from the time he was 12, pushing him to take risk after risk, expecting more and more of him, the pressure always mounting, the payback situations continually produced, until he finally became what his father wanted, a brutal extension of himself that he could manipulate and control forever.

And even when he'd broken away from him, he hadn't, not really. He'd viewed every figure of authority as just another tyrant like his father, so he spit in the tyrant's face, beginning with Bryson and ending with the Feds, while his father stayed behind getting increasingly crazy while still wielding power in Bobby's head.

How ironic it was, he thought, that getting caught the first time for slashing the coach's tires had resulted in being left out in the cold, shunned and isolated in that big open field under a gray and merciless sky. He'd prayed to God that day to help him out of his misery, to warm him from the cold. When his prayer went unanswered, he'd blamed it on himself, believing that God had witnessed his terrible deeds and was shunning him, too. That was the last time he had prayed until his prayer of gratitude after Sean Devereux made the deal for his sentence reduction.

The conviction had been the result of his second time getting caught, only that time he'd been sent to prison, away from the real punishment, the crushing blows of his father's disapproval and rejection, and found within the enclosure of prison walls the approval and acceptance he'd so desperately craved and the blessing of grace that had come to him in a vision of pure light. But it was the memory of his grandmother that was most recurrent in his mind now and lit the flame that was burning inside of him, the flame that was sparking his rebellion. The memory of her was with him now almost every day, and he could feel her love. He didn't need it from his father anymore.

His rebellion would be against the darkness that he had been forced to live in before he knew how to escape it, the life he hadn't chosen, the crimes he never wanted to commit. When he'd asked his grandmother to tell him more about the Cherokee renegades she compared him to, she'd described them as rebel warriors of wild nature, fierce and bold, who were fighting for their survival in the only way they knew how; they believed the fight to be a noble one, and in the end they had won their place in the forest. He thought of her words now as a prophecy, it was as if she knew that he would one day have to fight for his own survival, and she had tried to prepare him, placing the thought in his mind that he was capable of something noble in that fight. She must have also feared that he might become a renegade in the worst sense of the word, being the wise woman that she was, so she gave him an explanation of its meaning that held hope in it and the image had stayed with him as she prayed it would. She must have known that he would need it one day, and he did, be-cause now he *would* be her wild renegade once more, fighting for a life she would approve of, with the unencumbered noble heart he felt inside, pumping strong and bold.

Only this time, there would be no overpowering paternal ogre to draw him away from her love and influence. As a small boy, the power of this man had seemed awesome, and he'd been attracted to him like a magnet, born of him, part of him. What a fine figure of a man to have for a father, the way he walked and his manner of talking, his deep voice and the way others would look at him, the way people responded to everything he said, to be this man's boy, his only son, seemed a grand thing. He'd wanted to be with him as early as he could remember. As safe and happy as he'd felt in the home of his grandparents, he was pulled back to his parent's home, not by force but because he wanted to go there, wanted to be with his father. And even in the first awareness that something was amiss, that instinctual feeling that something was not quite right, he'd followed along, excited at the prospect of being with him. As a toddler he had followed him from room to room and then from indoors into the wondrous outdoors, where his father was a king, a master of the wilderness, a leader among men.

From the limited frame of reference of a child, he couldn't comprehend his first feelings of apprehension, the queasiness in his stomach, the uncertainty he felt when his father did something that didn't fit in with his idea of him, when excitement had turned into fear and his adoration had turned into aversion, and then his father had turned on him. The giant of a man he had once seemed became a giant of a nightmare, and it had happened so gradually throughout his formative years, when he was just a boy, just a boy.

But he was a boy no longer and knew now that he had been up against the most fearsome of them all and could take on any comers. That was why his grandmother had chosen a fearsome warrior for him to identify with. He would use the image to project strength during his remaining time in prison, but it would be contained and deflective. If he had to fight, he would, but not with vengeance or hatred. If he had to defend himself, he would, but not with intent to destroy. He would attempt to be righteous, fuel his brain with right-living teachings and principles, and fight the demons of his guilty conscience by not adding to his misdeeds.

Bobby used his vivid imagination to help him through the next three years. But Johnny G helped him to mature. He encouraged Bobby to learn about things other than his Bible without trying to sway him from it. Probably the most important thing he did was reflect back to Bobby what his real talents were and encourage him to think about a future in which he could put them to good use. Bobby had spent many hours describing to him his methods of hunting and fishing and tracking and skinning, his survival skills and knowledge of the forest. Johnny asked him if he'd ever considered being a legal hunting guide to sportsmen. Bobby wondered if it was even possible. He'd been on the illegal side of hunting for most of his life and hadn't considered the possibility of making an honest living at it. In fact, he hadn't thought much about any occupation other than "going straight." And that was a promise, not a plan.

There were days when he would rise early and stand at the

window of their upper floor room, gazing out through wire mesh covering at the countryside and woodlands and fields of Kentucky bluegrass. One windy morning, the fields were particularly beautiful, the grasses high and uncut, swaying in the shifting winds. One of the fields seemed like a river cutting through the others, lower and extending in length toward a patch of woodland, like the river in many ways with waves of ever-changing movement. He became mesmerized by the sweeping motion of its grasses bending softly and to and fro, the colors changing from pale green to greenish blue to golden green-brown in the morning light. His mountain spirit became restless and he yearned for the forest and streams, the only place on earth he called home.

Suddenly, a deer sprinted from the woodland into the field, stopped, then looked in his direction. As if in a trance, he saw himself sitting in a truck that had a dog box on the back with hounds inside of it and a rifle up in the back window, a 30-06 model 742 carbine. He was on a logging road on his way to a bear hunt, the two-way radio was on and there was a back and forth connection to coordinate the hunt with others who were participating. Then the truck was moving and up ahead, a black bear came running out of a forest into the road and crossed it before he could get a shot at it. After he missed his shot at the bear, he turned and looked back and could see himself in prison looking out the window. And then he was back at the window looking at nothing but the grasses blowing in the wind.

He'd seen a glimpse into the future but thought it to be more of a dream than a reality. The reality ahead for him was probation. He would have to serve three and a half years of probation after his six years served, and he could not have so much as a pellet gun or a bow and arrow, much less what he would need for a hunt.

Day followed day and month followed month and Bobby made it through his time without incident, even after Johnny G's release. By that time Johnny G had tutored him well in what to expect and how to get through it and then how to get through his years of probation. He was determined to abide by the rules, found a place to live in West Asheville, and stayed away from old haunts and negative influences. He found a job in an outfitter fly fishing shop in nearby Weaverville and began working out in a gym after work. There he met new friends, one of which was a young man named Tony.

Tony was a college student who would sometimes get discouraged about the years it was taking to earn his degree and the cost of his education. Bobby talked to him about doing time in the way he had and encouraged him to stick it out. Tony had never met someone who had served time, but he admired Bobby for his willingness to reveal that part of his life to help him and more so for his manner, physical strength and skill with martial arts. They were nothing alike and yet had struck up a friendship. Bobby listened to Tony, his frustrations and ambitions, and felt compelled to mentor him in some way. He continually encouraged Tony to hang in there and used himself as an example, saying things like, "You've got to stay in school. You don't want to end up like me. You're smart, but don't think you're too smart for an education, that's a mistake."

He tried to listen and talk to Tony the way Johnny had with him, and he felt good when Tony actually took his advice. It was a new role for him and made him feel more of a man than his previous methods of proving his manhood. During this time he was also dealing with his father, who had been diagnosed with Alzheimer's disease. Although he was in the care of professionals due to his State Department insurance benefits, he was an unruly patient as one might expect, with periods of rational thinking that would result in lenient confinement followed by strict confinements that tested the limits of those responsible for his care, despite the medications he was given. Bobby helped as much as he could but found it extremely stressful and had to be cautious about the time he spent with his father. There were moments when his father's former self would rear his head like a serpent and strike, injecting his poisonous venom into Bobby's heart. When that happened, Bobby envisioned the warrior, accepted the pain without allowing himself to harden inside, and took his leave, making sure of his father's care and trying to do his duty in the best way he could.

Interacting with his father made his probation time go slower and sometimes he drank alcohol, and sometimes too much, and he had to overcome the tendency. Then he got into a relationship that didn't work out and he had to recognize his mistake. But he stuck with his Bible and tried to do better, and one day his probation came to an end, and mercifully, so did his father.

The spring of that year, he was finally allowed to own a muzzle loader that enabled him to return to hunting and begin the life he'd been planning for almost ten years. He drove over to nearby Madison County to explore new hunting grounds. There was a place there he'd always been drawn to, an area in the county called Shelton Laurel where he'd visited with his father several times as a boy. Shelton Laurel was a land within a land, a place caught in time, a valley that ran almost 17 miles long and joined up with the North Carolina, Tennessee borderline 45 miles from west Asheville. He was convinced that he'd be better off away from Buncombe County and all the reminders of his past.

Shelton Laurel was known for its rugged terrain and clannish people. The valley was discovered around the 1790s during the time of the Revolutionary War by a group of indentured servants on the run. They formed a settlement within this inhospitable land of craggy rocks and scarce bottomland, undesirable for farming, because the land was cheap and cut off from the outside world. A community grew into an established settlement but reclusiveness became characteristic of the people there; they didn't take kindly to strangers and didn't easily accept anyone not born in the valley. They were standoffish, minded their own business, and created a haven within a rugged wilderness that remained somewhat backward but also protected from worse elements that had blossomed in more prosperous civilized areas. It was those elements that Bobby wanted to escape from and he thought of Shelton Laurel as the perfect spot to begin his new life. It was a rough, tough mountain paradise and a hunter's dream.

So he obtained a license to hunt there and on his first day out killed a wild turkey, which was quite an accomplishment with a muzzle loader, not easy to do. He took it as a sign from his grandmother and felt he was on the right track. But there would be other signs, and he came to believe that a plan had been designed for him rather than the other way around. He started looking for property on the edge of the valley near the forest area where hunting was permitted. He eventually found a parcel of land he could afford with an old mobile home on it, nestled into pines and off to itself, exactly what he needed.

He started staying there on days and weekends when he didn't have to work and enjoyed the freedom tremendously, exploring the surrounding forest, hunting and making trails, learning everything he could about the environment, studying the wildlife and searching for signs of black bear. He was a master woodsman, with instincts inherited from his father. He could live off the land in the forest and survive for days at a time with nothing but the clothes on his back, a pocket knife, and a lighter, and could make a fire without one if he had to.

He got to know some of the people who came around slowly and he didn't push it. He understood them and felt they would accept him in time. He reached a point where he wanted to stay there all the time. He had started collecting the equipment he would need and some of the weapons he would use, but there were many more things he needed and his funds were limited. He came upon one of his most essential needs by accident one day on a trail he'd discovered leading from the backwoods of his trailer toward the valley. Quite out of the blue, there appeared on the trail a half-starved stray dog that he identified as a Red-Tick English hound. The dog walked right up to him, had no collar, appeared to be lost, and was so thin that his ribs could be counted. Bobby took him back to the trailer, fed him and then put up a notice in the local post office, knowing that this breed of dog cost a lot of money. Weeks went by and the dog went with him everywhere, riding in the truck by his side and running ahead of him on the trails. Bobby couldn't believe his good fortune. No one ever claimed him. Bobby named him Red, and Red became his first bear dog.

With Red, he had another beginning but Red would also lead him somewhere even more providential. It happened the day Red disappeared from the trail and did not return. By that time, Bobby had grown attached to the dog and thought that Red had become attached to him. He searched for hours to no avail and called his name until he was hoarse. Feeling dejected and worried, he then went back to the trailer hoping that Red would be waiting for him there. But the dog was not there and Bobby felt aggrieved by his absence. That day seemed an eternity; he hadn't realized the depth of his need for companionship, having convinced himself that he was better off being a loner. And then, just before dark, his cell phone rang and he heard the voice of a woman telling him that she had his dog, had read the phone number from his tag. She gave him directions; she lived over the ridge not far from where the trail from his property led down to the valley. For some reason, Red had left him to take that trail and it was the one place he hadn't searched for him.

Her farmhouse was secluded, the property set back off a gravel road that ran along the outskirts of Shelton Laurel valley and its main roads. When he pulled up in his truck, she was waiting for him outside with Red standing beside her, as if he belonged there, as if he were her dog. She was open and friendly and invited him inside. She explained how the dog had come up to her while she was working in her garden that late afternoon. She'd noticed his tag when he allowed her to pet him and she'd taken him inside, fed him, and then made the call. Her name was Kate and she had the most beautiful hazel green eyes he'd ever seen and a way about her that made him feel welcome.

He asked her how long she'd lived in the valley. She said she'd only been there a few years, had visited the area during her teens, staying at a volleyball camp in one of Shelton Laurel's outdoors camp facilities. She'd thought it wildly beautiful and had always felt compelled to come back, finally did, wanting to start her life anew. She said her spirit had urged her to get off the grid and create her own environment away from the cities and crowds. He could see that she had, her farmhouse was primitive but attractive, cozy and warm. She grew organic vegetables and canned them for winter. Dried herbs hung in the kitchen and other roots and dried flowers. She had no TV, read lots of books instead. They ended up talking for hours and he knew he would return.

It was the catalyst he needed to step out and start up his business. He drove back to Asheville and had some business cards made with the heading, *Bobby Burris Professional Bear Hunter* against a scenic backdrop of Blue Ridge Mountains, a large black bear off to the side. He gave notice to his employer but left on good terms. He had made friends while working in the fly fishing store and the other outfitter stores in the area. They agreed to place his business cards on their poster boards. And they promised to send business his way, and he promised to reciprocate.

He spent the next two weeks trying to turn the mobile home into a functional base of operations. He collected his gear and equipment and organized his weaponry and belongings. And then he went back to Kate and started helping her around the farm, cutting wood and weeding the garden, bringing her fresh game, which, amazing to him, she helped him skin and cook. He'd never known a woman like her. She was a physical therapist by profession and worked at the local hospital four days a week to support her life on the farm. She was beautiful and feminine and yet strong and resourceful. She had an independent spirit and a love for nature and the good earth. She gave her place a new name, *Silver Lining Farm,* and with his help started raising chickens and ducks and goats. Bobby kept her stocked up with wood and game and helped take care of the farm animals. Red settled in on the porch and watched them fall in love.

He prayed the business would get off to a good start, despite his limited supplies. It wasn't as much of a gamble as it might have been in his father's day. Things had changed since that period when the bear population had diminished and the bears had gone to high ground. According to the North Carolina Wildlife Department, the bear population in Western North Carolina had significantly grown in recent years, along with the simultaneous encroachment of humans into bears' natural habitats. A prolonged regional drought had also reduced the food supply for bears causing them to leave their natural habitats to hunt for sustenance.

The bears were coming in closer and closer as developments were being carved out wherever land could be purchased. The Blue Ridge Mountains had become a retirement Mecca and a major tourist attraction since the opening of the Blue Ridge Parkway. The retired wealthy and famous wanted private mountain retreats built aloft ridges and precipices that afforded the most scenic views. Land developers were building gated communities and golf resorts and expensive condominiums in places even the mountain people wouldn't have tried to settle.

The black bears that once shied away from the settlement areas were getting more aggressive and destructive, less fearful of man. There were increased reported incidents of bear attacks, extensive property damage, and many sightings in campgrounds, towns and villages. People were constantly warned to keep food stored properly when camping and garbage cans sealed tightly near their homes. The wildlife departments had amended bear hunting regulations and sportsmen were eager to take advantage of them. However, bear hunting was a dangerous sport and hunters with experience were needed to help with the problem and to assist as guides.

Although it was a good time for Bobby to begin his business, he was beginning with the bare essentials. But he'd prepared himself in the most important ways by becoming acquainted with every law and ordinance regarding his profession and making a good impression on other hunters with whom he came in contact. They were his best referral source and he connected with them by placing his business cards in gun and sporting shops whenever he went into town. A card he put up at the Spring Bluff Mountain Shop resulted in a call from a Madison County hunter by the name of Seth Bradley. Seth was not a prospective client but had done some bear hunting and was looking for someone to hunt with who might teach him more about it. Most of Seth's buddies hunted deer and other game and avoided hunting bear because of the risk involved.

Bobby and Seth struck up a friendship and they went hunting together several times. Seth offered to help Bobby build his bear dog pack from his own pack and also offered his assistance on hunts. Seth had all of the equipment needed for a successful hunt, but Bobby had the expertise and know-how that Seth admired. They continued to hunt together, preparing for new clients. They placed tracking devices on the dogs, set up a two-way radio system for coordinating the hunts, and developed a network of friends in the area. Bobby learned from Seth a lot about the bear population in the Madison County region and why some of his buddies were afraid to go after them. He told Bobby, "They're not like anything else, man. They'll kill you, and they ain't afraid of nothin' anymore. They're moving in our direction to get away from all the construction and all those god-damned people who keep aggravating them and they keep on populating like they's trying to get more power."

Bobby wasn't afraid. He knew he was born to it. Bear hunting was in his blood and there weren't many like him anymore. Even Seth had come to see that Bobby had a sixth sense for locating bear habitat and he seemed to have eyes in the back of his head when tracking one down. If Seth was going to test himself hunting bear, he wanted to do it with a hunter like Bobby. He just wanted to be part of his plan.

Bobby didn't believe he had a plan anymore and the life he was leading had been given to him every step of the way. Then the calls started coming and before long Bobby and Seth were taking high level top-of-the-line outfitted sportsmen into the forest on a regular basis, men that reminded him of CB. Bobby made sure to give them the adventure they were seeking, a special experience each time, and he gave it to them with all his heart and soul.